Ethics since 1900

OPUS I   *Oxford Paperbacks University Series*

MARY WARNOCK

Ethics since 1900

Second Edition

London
OXFORD UNIVERSITY PRESS
New York Toronto
1966

Oxford University Press, Ely House, London W·1
GLASGOW NEW YORK TORONTO MELBOURNE WELLINGTON
CAPE TOWN SALISBURY IBADAN NAIROBI LUSAKA ADDIS ABABA
BOMBAY CALCUTTA MADRAS KARACHI LAHORE DACCA
KUALA LUMPUR HONG KONG

First edition in the Home University Library *1960*
Reprinted 1961 and 1963
Second edition in Oxford Paperbacks University Series *1966*

PRINTED IN GREAT BRITAIN
BY BUTLER & TANNER LTD, FROME AND LONDON

Contents

Preface

IN A BOOK OF THIS KIND the accident of where and when the author was educated is bound to make a difference, both to the selection and the treatment of the material. I am aware of numbers of omissions; and doubtless prejudice appears on every page. I have not been able to discuss all the philosophers who have contributed towards the different kinds of moral philosophy current in the last sixty years. Some of the omissions are made good in the bibliography, but this is, I realize, no substitute for a full treatment of their arguments.

It may be thought that in some cases too long has been spent on the details of a rather trivial argument, at the expense of a wider view of the whole subject. My defence would be that in a subject such as ethics, the details of the arguments are all-important. Conclusions are valueless and positively misleading without some at least of the reasoning which led up to them being set out.

I have not, I hope, had any preconceived idea of what ethics is. I have discussed what seem to me the most important contributions to philosophy which have been made roughly under that heading; there could, of course, be very different selections. I have purposely left out all political philosophy, although aware that it is sometimes very closely connected with ethics.

Finally, it hardly needs saying that no problems are settled in this book; but I should like to think that perhaps some questions, though they are not raised for the first time, are at least re-opened. It is agreeable to reflect that there is a great deal of moral philosophy still to be written.

1

Metaphysical Ethics: F. H. Bradley

AT THE BEGINNING of the twentieth century ethics was predominantly metaphysical. The most important writers on moral philosophy explicitly linked their discussions of morals with views about the nature of the universe as a whole, and man's place in the universe. A *system* of ethics was what such philosophers aimed to set out, and this meant a total explanation of the way things are, which contained as part of itself an explanation of the demands and the requirements of ethical behaviour. In thus basing ethics upon metaphysics, English writers, at least, were defending the subject against the blows they thought had been dealt to it by Hume, Bentham, Mill, and the utilitarians. For instance, in 1925 A. E. Taylor, himself a metaphysician, wrote an essay entitled 'The Freedom of Man'.[1] In it he listed the most important of his immediate predecessors in the subject: T. H. Green, the Cairds, Nettleship, William Wallace, Adamson, Bosanquet, Bradley; and he said: 'The chief part of their united work was to continue the age-long war of believers in genuine morality and real obligation against every kind of naturalistic substitute.' Naturalism was supposed to explain away ethics altogether by associating ethical concepts such as goodness or duty with non-ethical concepts such as pleasure or utility or the desire that society should be preserved. It was believed that metaphysical ethics could reinstate the subject by demonstrating the necessary uniqueness and irreducibility of these ethical concepts.

[1] *Contemporary British Philosophy*, 2nd Series. Edited by J. H. Muirhead. Allen & Unwin, London, 1925.

Of these metaphysical philosophers by far the most powerful was F. H. Bradley. His *Ethical Studies* was first published in 1876, but his views did not radically alter thereafter. In 1893 he explicitly referred to the book and said that it still, for the most part, represented his views; and in 1924 he started to revise, though not to re-write it. The second edition was published after his death, in 1927. It is fair, therefore, to count this as a book belonging to the twentieth century.

The second essay in *Ethical Studies* is entitled 'Why Should I be Moral?' In this Bradley states in outline his solution to what he thinks are the problems of ethics, the problems, that is, of the nature of the end for man, and of the supreme good. His solution is that the good is self-realization, and that this is the end or the purpose of the moral man's life. At first he seeks to establish this by an appeal to moral consciousness. He takes for granted that there is a certain set of facts with which everyone is acquainted, such as the fact that we often feel ourselves to be under some obligation, or that we often feel that morally we have failed in some way. To these facts, or rather our knowledge of them, he refers as moral consciousness. He raises no question about the scope of morality, or the application of moral concepts. These things are accepted as the data on which the moral philosopher has to work. This unquestioning attitude to the supposed facts of our moral life, and the appeal to such arbiters as 'pleasure', 'duty', 'moral consciousness', all absolutely in general, makes Bradley's writing seem at times fantastically abstract and difficult to connect with any single particular phenomenon. But in this generality also lies its power, since if his account seems explanatory at all, it seems explanatory of every aspect of life.

It is worth considering in a little more detail what he says in this second essay.[1] The question why I should be moral is, he says, illegitimate; for to ask it would suggest that there was some ulterior purpose behind the exercise of virtue, or the performance of duty. 'To take virtue as a mere means to an ulterior end is in direct antagonism to the voice of moral consciousness.' But in spite of this, later, in a footnote, Bradley does himself offer an answer to the question.[2] 'A man is moral because he

---

[1] *Ethical Studies*, p. 58.   [2] *op. cit.* footnote to p. 62.

likes being moral; and he likes it partly because he was brought up to the habit of liking it, and partly because he finds it gives him what he wants while its opposite does not do so.' This last statement looks practically tautological, but it does lead to Bradley's main solution to the problem of what is the end for human life. The most general expression for the end in itself is, he says, *self-realization*. It is to the amplification of this solution that the rest of the book is mainly devoted. His first attempt to prove the truth of the general statement comes in this same essay.[1] Once again he appeals to moral consciousness to 'see what it tells us about its end'. And he asks the ordinary reader to reflect whether we do not all aim not only at the realization of self, but of self as a whole. At first glance, it must be admitted, these words are not particularly lucid or revealing.

It is not clear what is meant by 'realizing' the self, let alone realizing it 'as a whole'. But though it is easy either to be put off by the unclarities, or to stop trying to understand, and simply to drift along with the style as one reads, it is all the same possible to detect in Bradley's theory something which is important and is very often at the back of people's minds when they talk about morality. Bradley thinks of people's wills, as opposed to their chance or random desires, as being directed over a period of time to a way of life, a system of interconnected actions. Everybody makes his own system, in the sense that no one else can exercise his will for him. His actions are necessarily his own and no one else's. Moreover, in the case of acts which would naturally be thought of as the concern of morality, not only is there something to be done, but the whole point, for the agent, is that it should be done *by him* and no one else. Thus a morally good or a morally bad act is a kind of self-assertion or self-expression. It is, in fact, not merely a tautology that a man's acts are his own; for when we judge a man's acts from a moral point of view it is as *his* acts, part of his whole system of actions, that we judge them. Our judgement might have been different if someone else had done the same thing, or brought about the same consequences. Bradley takes this to be a difference between moral action and acts of artistic production. In producing a work of art someone might believe that there was something which

[1] *op. cit.* pp. 65 *sqq.*

had to be done, a certain aesthetic result to be achieved. In morality an action has to be done, too, but not as a means to a result. The doing of it *by me*, he says, can actually be considered as the end. He does not, in this essay, do more than suggest this contrast between the aesthetic and the moral, and I do not think that it would bear much looking into, at any rate as a criterion for distinguishing them. But it does throw light, perhaps, on the kind of thing that is meant by self-realization. Furthermore it serves to direct our attention to what was for Bradley the most important feature of morality . . . its essential dynamism. The moral world is a world of active agents, choosing things and doing things, and projecting themselves upon their environment. He says:

For morality, the end implies the act, and the act implies self-realization. This if it were doubtful, would be shown . . . by the feeling of pleasure which attends the putting forth of the act. For if pleasure be the feeling of self, and accompany the act, this indicates that the putting forth of the act is also the putting forth of the self.

So far, the concept of self-realization seems to be connected first with the concept of dynamism as the essential element in the moral life, and, secondly, with the concept of character. To be truly moral or immoral, our actions must in some sense be consistent. They must arise, that is, out of a consistent character, and manifest that character. This is in fact a very important part of morality and enters more than is often allowed into our moral judgement of others. Moreover, as so far stated, the self-realization theory has another great advantage. Many people, especially those who are temperamentally puritanical, or who are used to setting very high standards for themselves, feel strongly that some kinds of behaviour, though utterly harmless to other people, should nevertheless be avoided for their own sakes, and that this is a moral matter. They may feel, for instance, that to indulge in some kinds of pleasurable activities such as reading novels in the mornings, is wrong, not only because they have been brought up to think this, but because they feel that to indulge in them would be to start some kind of downward trend, some degeneration which it is their duty to avoid. The feeling that, consequences apart, one should do better, is a strong and familiar moral feeling and one which is, again, unduly neglected by writers about morals. Self-realization is not so far from self-improvement, and it is, among other things, in its power to account for this range of moral concepts that the attraction of Bradley's theory lies.

But Bradley, as I have said already, claims that the aim of morality is not only realization of the self, but of the self *as a whole*. This part of his doctrine is both less clear, and less attractive, if I understand it. In the essay we are now considering he makes two serious attempts to elucidate the concept of the self as a whole. The first is by means of an analysis of a choice between two incompatible alternative actions.[1] He says that in choosing between A and B not only must a man be aware of the nature of the acts between which he is choosing, but he must also be aware of himself set above these two actions and deliberating between them. This self-awareness he denominates the universal element in volition, the particular element being the agent's awareness of each of the individual possibilities. The volition *as a whole* is the identification of the self willing with one or other of the possible actions; and this resulting unity, that is, the volition completed in an action, he calls the individual whole, or the concrete universal. It is at achieving such a whole that the moral action aims, and this is what is meant by saying that the end is self-realization *as a whole*. I cannot pretend, however, that the necessity of talking about the whole is made any more apparent by this obscure Hegelian reasoning, nor, in particular, that the relation between the whole volition and the whole self is obvious.

The second attempted elucidation, also purely Hegelian, is by means of an analogy with understanding.[2] In matters of theory our aim, he says, is to understand an object, to 'get at the truth of it'. As long as the object seems odd or unfamiliar we say that we have not reached the truth about it. We go on until we can see the consistency and the necessity of some explanatory theory of the object. 'There we rest, because then we have found the nature of our own mind and the truth of facts in one.' If ever our knowledge of anything were complete, the distinction between the knowing mind and the object known would disappear. It is towards this identification of subject with object that Bradley

[1] *op. cit.* p. 71. [2] *op. cit.* p. 73.

thinks we strive, in trying to understand anything. There is an analogous striving, he claims, in the case of action. 'Here our aim is not, leaving the given as it is, to find the truth of it; but here we want to force the sensuous fact to correspond to the truth of ourselves.' The distinction at removing which we aim in practice is the distinction between ourselves and the alien world of other people and external events. 'My nature tells me that the world is mine'; and therefore I try to alter the facts, till I express myself in *them* as well as in what first seemed distinct from them. The aim is to find in the facts 'nothing but myself carried out'. I possess the world when my will is expressed in the world.

The idea that knowing implies some kind of identification between the person who knows and the known object has of course a long and serious metaphysical history. Aristotle thought that there existed a kinship between the objects of intellectual comprehension and the intellect. Spinoza held that if one understood nature completely one would thereby become identical with nature, that is identical with God. Bradley regarded the unitary nature of reality as both the most important and the least dubitable part of his whole metaphysical account of the universe; and he meant his statement that reality was one to carry the implication, among others, that anything less than unity, such as the distinction between a person and the object of his thought, is necessarily unreal or illusory. To aim, therefore, at identifying oneself, whether with the object of one's thought or with the world in which one is living and acting, is to do no more than to aim to remove illusion, and to exist in reality. In this context, self-realization takes on a more literal sense than at first it seemed to have. It means now not only satisfying oneself, but actually making oneself exist. It means making oneself real instead of illusory. Furthermore, the notion that the self must be realized *as a whole* becomes a necessary part of its being realized at all, since if there is more than one thing, or rather if there is less than total identification between myself and the world around me, then the realization is not complete; if it is complete, then myself and the world form one whole. Thus moral action will not only remove the *sense* of isolation or separateness which each one of us may have, but it will, on this theory, actually bring such separateness to an end.

So, by restating his moral theory in the context of the idealist theory of knowledge, Bradley attempts to elucidate his utterance, that the aim of moral action is self-realization. At the end of this same essay he adds the qualification that not only must the self be realized as a whole, but as an infinite whole.[1] This too, presumably, follows from the proposition that reality is one; it follows, at least, on the hypothesis that reality is infinite, which Bradley doubtless accepted. But it is impossible not to feel, at this stage of the argument, that any application of the theory to what are normally thought of as the peculiar problems of moral philosophy has been left rather alarmingly far behind. In this essay, Bradley only hints at any such application, at the very end:[2]

The difficulty is: being limited and so not a whole, how extend myself so as to be whole? The answer is, be a member in a whole. Here your private self, your finitude, ceases as such to exist; it becomes the function of an organism. You must be, not a mere piece of, but a member in, a whole; and as this, must know and will yourself.

This, though still vague as a guide to the nature of what is morally good, has at least a slightly sinister note. There is the suggestion that the end for man, self-realization, may turn out after all to be the destruction of the individual.

The next two essays in *Ethical Studies* are critical considerations of other people's views of the nature of the end. First Bradley considers and rejects the suggestion that the end is pleasure, and then that it is duty for duty's sake. In each case he aims to show that the suggestion is actually contradictory. These essays, especially the second of them, are both subtle and forcible. No doubt, in Duty for Duty's sake, he is not entirely fair to Kant, but all the same this seems to me one of the very best things ever written about Kant's moral philosophy. In the fifth essay, 'My Station and its Duties',[3] he returns to his own theory, and to the task of illustrating the concept of self-realization in a more concrete form. The good for man is now definitely stated to be 'the realization of ourselves as the will which is above ourselves'. This will is identical with a 'moral organism'. It is

[1] *op. cit.* p. 74.   [2] *op. cit.* p. 79.   [3] *op. cit.* pp. 160 *sqq.*

referred to as a concrete universal which cannot exist except in and through its members. The individual, Bradley says, must necessarily be thought of as having relations with other people. He is not born into a vacuum, but has a definite place in society and in history. Whatever he does must be done in relation to the circumstances into which he was born, and it is with this external world that he tries to identify himself, by altering the facts until they express himself. This view, the belief in the necessary dependence of people upon one another and upon their circumstances, is set out in explicit opposition in the first place to individualism, that is to utilitarianism interpreted as a kind of egoistic hedonism, and secondly to the Kantian and abstract formulae of Duty for Duty's sake. The theory of self-realization as a part of a moral organism, the theory which Bradley actually refers to by the name of 'My Station and its Duties', is said to have three great advantages. First, the universal end for man which is proposed by it is concrete. The theory takes into account actual facts and is therefore prepared to allow that duty will not be the same at every time or place. In this Bradley thinks it is superior to both hedonism and the abstract view. But though the end proposed is concrete, he claims that it is not given by mere caprice, 'for although within certain limits I may choose my station according to my own liking, yet I and everyone else must have some station with duties pertaining to it, and those duties do not depend on our opinion or liking'. Secondly, the end is objective, and this is one of the demands which the moral consciousness makes upon anything that could qualify to be an end. The reasons which Bradley gives to support this claim of objectivity are, it must be confessed, less than clear. The justification appears to be that the objective, systematized moral organism, which is not something each of us just thinks up for himself, is the medium through which the individual man must realize the end.[1]

My private choice, so far as I am moral, is the mere form of bestowing myself on, and identifying myself with, the will of the moral organism, which realizes in its process both itself and myself. . . . What I have to do, I have not to force upon a recalcitrant world; I have to fill my place—the place that waits for me to fill it.

[1] *op. cit.* p. 180.

The third advantage of 'My Station and its Duties' is said to be that the end which it proposes leaves nothing of us outside it. It gets rid of the contradiction which Bradley found in the Kantian theory of pure duty, the contradiction, that is, between duty and the empirical self of desires, inclination, character and circumstances. All these, as we have seen, are included in the end, on Bradley's theory, since duty now becomes the duty to make all these empirical elements part of the wider external world.

The concept of 'My Station and its Duties' is the core of Bradley's moral theory. The last two essays in *Ethical Studies* are devoted to further elaboration of this notion of the end, to a consideration of the bad will, the opposite of self-realization, and to a discussion of the relation between religion and morality. The respects in which the theory is essentially metaphysical are perhaps now clear. More specifically, it is essentially an idealist moral philosophy, deriving from the idealist view of the unitary and coherent nature of reality. In *Appearance and Reality*[1] Bradley returns to the question of The Good. Here the connexion between the concept of goodness and that of reality as a whole is most clearly stated, and ethics is seen as a small part of metaphysics. Evil and good, he says, are not illusions but they are appearances, 'they are one-sided aspects, each over-ruled and transmuted in the whole'.[2] The opposition between good and bad is not supposed to be absolute, any more than, on the idealist theory, is the opposition between true and false absolute. 'The interval which exists between, and which separates, the lower and the higher, is measured by the idea of perfect Reality. The lower is that which, to be made complete, would have to undergo a more total transformation of its nature.' If, in general, then, the more good anything is the more reality it has, it follows that in the sphere of action, the better an action is, the more reality will it bestow upon the agent. Self-realization is only one aspect of the general superior reality of things as they approach closer and closer to *absolute* reality (in so far, that is, as they improve). Moreover, the good man will necessarily realize himself in a wide context; his actions will necessarily take their place in a whole system of morality, because what he is aiming at

---

[1] Sonnenschein, London, 1st edition, 1893.
[2] *op. cit.* pp. 401 *sqq.*

in exercising his good will, is, in some sense, to comprehend and identify himself with everything that exists.

Bradley was not, of course, the only metaphysical moral philosopher of this period. Nor was he even interested in all the problems which seemed important to his contemporaries. For instance he was comparatively uninterested in the problem of human freedom. It seems probable that this lack of interest was due to the fact that there was really no place for freedom in his system, which, like Spinoza's, must entail that the more we know, the more we realize that our actions are a necessary part of the total system of the universe. Just as good and bad are not opposed except as appearances, so voluntary and necessitated would only *appear* to our ignorance to be opposed. Any believer in an idealist theory of truth almost has to hold that ultimately everything is necessary. There were other metaphysical philosophers, however, such as A. E. Taylor, who conceived of the problem of freedom as the central ethical problem, and who attacked Bradley for overlooking it. Again, Joseph, in *Some Problems of Ethics* (1931), starts with a chapter called 'Metaphysical Preliminaries', which is entirely devoted to the question whether or not we may say that any human actions are voluntary. All the same, it was Bradley's Hegelian idealist ethical theory which dominated the beginning of the century, and it is against this background that the later developments must be seen. In ethics, as in philosophy in general, the greatest blow to be struck in the twentieth century against idealism was struck by G. E. Moore. And though in *Principia Ethica*, which will be the subject of the next chapter, he had other targets as well as Bradley and the idealists, it was his arguments against them and therefore, it seemed, against metaphysical ethics in general, which were most novel, and which perhaps have had the greatest influence on twentieth-century ethics as a whole.

2
G. E. Moore

G. E. MOORE'S *Principia Ethica* was first published in 1903. It has become the custom to regard it as the source from which the subsequent moral philosophy of the century has flowed, or at least as the most powerful influence upon this moral philosophy. There is no doubt that it is a very remarkable book. But I am not sure that some later writers have not submitted to the temptation of seeing in it only what they would themselves subscribe to, and of leaving out of account altogether those features of the book which are idiosyncratic and eccentric. This is a pity; Moore has, no doubt, exercised a great influence on other philosophers. But it is almost as if some of these philosophers, especially some in Oxford, had read only the first one or two chapters of the book; if they had read on, they might have been more cautious about ranging themselves under Moore's supposed banner.

In the Preface to *Principia Ethica*, Moore states what his main intention was in writing the book. 'I have tried,' he says, 'to distinguish clearly two kinds of question, which moral philosophers have always professed to answer, but which . . . they have almost always confused both with one another and with other questions.' These two questions are 'What kind of things ought to exist for their own sake?' and 'What kind of actions ought we to perform?' From knowing the answers to these two different questions, Moore says, we shall be able to go on to find out with what kind of evidence, if any, it is proper to support moral judgements; we shall know what kinds of ethical proposition are, and what kinds are not, susceptible of proof. In

general, Moore's answer to his questions is this: (1) The things
which ought to exist for their own sake are things which we call
intrinsically good. It is impossible to define 'good', since it is the
name of a simple unanalysable characteristic of things. But this
does not entail that we cannot recognize when we see them those
things which intrinsically possess this unanalysable characteristic. Moore's contention is that we can, if we think about it
hard enough, certainly recognize intrinsically good things, and
at the end of the book he lists some of the things which he
thinks are intrinsically good. But it is a matter simply of recognition. No evidence can be adduced to show that something is
intrinsically good; it is just a matter of seeing that it is so.
Nothing could *prove* that if something is said to be intrinsically
good, it really is so. 'We can guard against error only by taking
care, that, when we try to answer a question of this kind, we have
before our minds that question only and not some other or
others' (p. viii). (2) Answers to the second question, what kinds
of action ought we to perform, are capable of proof or disproof,
of an empirical sort. For we ought always to do that action which
will cause most good to exist. So the kind of evidence necessary
to show that some proposed course of action is right will be
causal evidence that the course of action will bring about such
and such results or consequences. In addition, it will be necessary to know that the consequences are intrinsically good. It is
necessary, therefore, on Moore's view, first to know what kinds
of things are intrinsically good, that is what kind of things
ought in general to exist, before it is possible to embark on any
demonstration that a certain course of action ought to be undertaken, since the evidence brought up to support this last contention must contain some statement of the former kind.

This, then, is what Moore took to be the main purpose of his
book, namely to distinguish those ethical judgements which
were susceptible of proof by reference to evidence from those
which were not. The first step in establishing this distinction
was to consider the concept of goodness, in order to show that
'good' was simple and indefinable, and to this consideration the
first chapter of the book is devoted. In this chapter Moore ex-
pounds his famous theory that it is fallacious to attempt to
define 'good' in any way, and, particularly, fallacious to attempt

to define it in terms of a natural object. Moore calls the attempt
to define 'good', which is indefinable, The Naturalistic Fallacy.
But it is important to notice that the fallaciousness consists in the
attempting of a definition at all, rather than specifically in
defining a so-called non-natural object in terms of a natural
object. Moore says (p. 13) that if anyone confused two natural
objects together, and defined one in terms of the other, this
would be to commit the very same fallacy as that contained in
the attempt to define good, only in this case there would be no
reason to call the fallacy 'naturalistic'. The appropriateness of
that name does come from mixing the two classes, natural and
non-natural; but even if 'good' were a natural object 'that would
not alter the nature of the fallacy, nor diminish its importance
one whit'. It is clear, then, that first and foremost it is supposed
to be fallacious to define 'good' and secondly it is fallacious to
define a non-natural in terms of a natural object. I have laboured
this point, not without reason. For people often talk not only as
if Moore were interested in nothing except exposing a logical
fallacy for its own sake, but also as if the nature of this fallacy
were simply to confuse a natural with a non-natural object, to
define the latter in terms of the former. And it must be admitted that the name 'Naturalistic Fallacy' does carry this
suggestion. But Moore does not care much for the name. 'It
does not matter what we call it provided we recognize it when
we meet it.' The true fallacy is the attempt to define the indefinable.

There are several obscure points in this doctrine as so far
expounded. Some of them, it must be admitted, must remain
obscure, but I will try to set out Moore's argument as clearly as
I can.

Moore distinguishes three possible meanings of the question
'What is good?' First, it may require a particular answer.
Obviously in this sense the question would not in fact be put in
this general form, but would be of the form, for instance, of
'Which is a good restaurant?' or 'What would be a good way to
begin a speech?' So I think we may dismiss this supposed
meaning of the question. The second meaning is that in which
the question requires a general answer in the form of a statement that some kind of thing is good—such as that charitable

actions are good or pleasure is good. Moore, at the end of the book, proposes answers to this version of the question. Thirdly, the question 'What is good?' may be the demand for a *definition*. In this form, Moore says that the question is absolutely central to ethics, and belongs to ethics alone. But by 'definition' it should be noticed that Moore here means 'analysis'. He dismisses the suggestion that he could reach the kind of definition demanded in the question 'What is good?' by observing how people in fact use the word 'good'. This kind of definition he regards as trivial, and a matter of mere lexicography. But, taking for granted that he is discussing the word 'good' in the way that it *is* usually used, he is interested in the object or idea which he says it is usually used to stand for. A definition, then, in the interesting sense, would be an analysis of this idea. It is this which he claims is impossible, in the case of the object denoted by 'good'. Moore's view of definition is very obscure, and his examples do not help to make it clearer. He contrasts the case of 'good' with the case of 'horse' (p. 8). The definition of 'horse' is said to be 'hooved quadruped of the genus equus'. This may be either (1) an arbitrary verbal definition telling you only how I propose to use the word, or (2) a statement about how English people do or should use the word 'horse', or (3) we may, Moore says, 'mean something much more important.' We may mean that a certain object familiar to all of us is composed in a certain manner. 'That it has four legs, a head, a heart, a liver etc. all of them arranged in definite relations to one another.' It is in this sense of definition that Moore denies that 'good' is definable. But it is difficult to see how the quoted definition of 'horse'—that it is a hooved quadruped of the genus equus—could ever be taken as *meaning* that the horse had a heart, liver etc. arranged in a certain order. No doubt one could list the parts of the horse, and even state their relation one to another, but to do this would not be to say 'hooved quadruped etc.', with a special meaning; nor would it normally be taken to be defining 'horse' at all. However, I do not think one should waste very much time on Moore's eccentric treatment of the word 'definition'. For one thing, the concept of definition is itself very vague, and it is not clear that anything very important would come of laying down the different ways in which things may or may not be defined. Furthermore, if we drop the word 'definition', and drop the confusing analogy of the horse, nothing much will be lost. For Moore makes it perfectly clear that what he thinks you cannot legitimately do to 'good' is to analyse it. It is impossible to name its parts because it has no parts. Like Descartes and Leibniz, Moore takes it as absolutely self-evident that if some things are complex and therefore capable of analysis, then there must be some things into which the complex things are analysed which are themselves simple, and without parts. This is a very widespread and natural belief. Moore thinks that the quality of goodness, which he talks of, confusingly, as 'good' either with or without inverted commas, is one of these simple natures which can enter into the composition of complexes, but are non-complex themselves. He compares goodness with yellowness in this respect (p. 10): 'Yellow and good, we say, are not complex: they are notions of that simple kind out of which definitions are composed and with which the power of further defining ceases.' 'Good' and 'bad', he says, are the only simple notions which are peculiar to ethics. The indefinability of 'good' is, he thinks, one of the most important facts, if not the most important fact, with which ethics has to deal. Again I quote:

If I am asked 'what is good?' my answer is that good is good and that is the end of the matter. Or if I am asked 'How is good to be defined?' my answer is that it cannot be defined, and that is all I have to say about it. But disappointing as these answers may appear, they are of the very last importance.

Having set out his contention that goodness, like yellowness, is unanalysable, Moore goes on to use the analogy between 'good' and 'yellow' to establish two further points. The first point is that though it is impossible to define colour words, it is possible to state the physical concomitants of the colours. We may state what light vibrations must strike the normal eye in order that the colour may be perceived. But, Moore says, these light vibrations are not what we mean when we talk about the colour. In this he is perfectly right. The colour word is the name of a property perceptible to the normal eye, not the name of something which it needs scientific measurement to discover. Similarly, Moore argues, with 'good', it may be possible to state what else besides being good all good things are; for instance it might turn out that if ever anything was good it was also pleasant, or the object of approval. But this would not entail that when we talked of a thing's being good, we *meant* that it was pleasant or the object of approval. In fact, if it were not possible independently to distinguish things which were good from those which were not, it would never be possible to find out that all the good things were also pleasant. To identify the light waves with the colour or the pleasantness with the goodness is to commit the fallacy of trying to define what is simple and indefinable. This argument, it will be seen, rests entirely on the assumption that 'good' is indeed like 'yellow', the name of a discernible property of things.

The second point which the analogy with colour is used to make is this: nobody thinks that because 'yellow' is indefinable, therefore it is impossible to say what things have the property of being yellow. Nor does anybody think that there can be only one thing which is yellow, nor that all the other properties which the yellow thing has are identical with the property of yellowness. We know perfectly well that primroses are yellow, that other things besides primroses are yellow, and that primroses are sweet-smelling as well as yellow, and that their sweet smell is different from their yellowness. Yet, Moore thinks, people have failed to see all these points when they have thought about the goodness of things. Saying that goodness is indefinable does not prevent one from saying that, for example, pleasure is good, that other things besides pleasure are good, and that pleasure may have other properties, such as being the object of desire, which are distinct from its goodness. This point is very important for Moore's argument, since his interest in ethics is by no means confined to the supposed logical point about the simplicity of certain concepts; he is interested in actually stating what things have the property of intrinsic goodness; in giving examples, that is, of his first, unprovable, kind of ethical proposition. This he plainly could not do unless he could show that it was possible to pick things out as possessors of the indefinable property of goodness.

So far Moore has given no arguments to show that 'good' is indefinable; there has been nothing except an analogy. He next attempts an actual proof, by means of a dilemma (p. 15). Either 'good' is indefinable, or, if it is not, it must be either a complex, about the correct analysis of which there could be disagreement, or the word must mean nothing at all. There is a certain amount of confusion here and elsewhere in the discussion, about whether we are supposed to be discussing a word or some object denoted by a word, such as a property; but this confusion is not very important, and Moore's dilemma can easily be presented in a way which avoids the difficulty. We must accept either that the word 'good' denotes a simple unanalysable property, or that it denotes a complex analysable property, or that it denotes nothing at all. This, Moore thinks, exhausts the possibilities. He then aims to show that each of the last alternatives is impossible, and that therefore we must necessarily accept the first. (1) 'The hypothesis that disagreement about the meaning of good is disagreement with regard to the correct analysis of a given whole, may be most plainly seen to be incorrect by consideration of the fact that, whatever definition be offered, it may be always asked, with significance, of the complex so defined whether it is itself good.' Thus, if I try to define good as, let us say, self-realization, Moore's objection is that it is still significant to ask whether self-realization is good; and since this is significant, it cannot be the same as asking whether self-realization is self-realization, which it would have to be if the original definition had been correct. One cannot doubt that self-realization is the same as self-realization; but we can and may well doubt whether self-realization is good, and the mere fact that we understand very well what is meant by doubting it, shows clearly that we have two different notions before our mind. This argument begs the question. For it already assumes what it is supposed to prove, namely, that goodness is simple and unanalysable. If goodness were allowed to be a complex notion, then not only might one perhaps be able to analyse it, but it would naturally be significant to convert the proposition and inquire whether that into which one had analysed it was good. This might well be a way of testing out the correctness of the analysis. An analysis of a complex notion never sets out to give an identity, nor is the statement in which the analysis is given an identity statement. Therefore the converse of the proposition in which the analysis

It is because he is convinced that each thing is what it is and not another thing!!

is set out will not be trivial. It is only because Moore is already convinced that 'good' is the name of a simple property that he thinks the possibility of significant conversion is fatal to the definition's being correct. This is clearly shown by the sentence quoted above. 'We have two different notions before our mind.' If the definition were correct, he thinks, we would have only one, as I might be said to have only one notion before my mind when I say that 'good' is '*bon*'. But if I can succeed in giving a correct analysis of a complex notion, then it cannot plausibly be said that I have only one notion before my mind; I must necessarily have at least two, and probably more. It is doubtful whether the method of counting the notions before the mind is a good or even possible method in fact. But if Moore requires that we use it, then for what it is worth, it must be admitted that it fails to prove what he wants it to. Moore seems to have been misled here by his own eccentric concept of definition. If he had used the word 'analysis', and had aimed to show that it is analysis of the concept of goodness which is impossible, then the argument from the possibility of converting any proposition of the form 'good is so and so' would not have seemed so formidable.

(2) The same considerations, Moore says, serve to show that 'good' is not totally meaningless. When anyone says that anything is good, Moore says, they are not saying nothing about it, nor are they saying something which can be paraphrased by another word. If, that is, I say that pleasure is good, I am not merely stating that pleasure is pleasure (a trivial proposition which would be saying nothing), nor am I saying something which could just as well be expressed by saying pleasure is, for instance, desired, or approved.

Everyone does in fact understand the question 'Is this good?' When he thinks of it, his state of mind is different from what it would be, were he asked 'Is this pleasant, or desired, or approved?' It has a distinct meaning for him, even though he may not recognize in what respect it is distinct. Whenever he thinks of intrinsic value or 'intrinsic worth' or says that a thing ought to exist, he has before his mind the unique object—the unique property of things—which I mean by 'good'.

This looks much more like a restatement of the position than an argument.

Both alternative possibilities having been thus ruled out, Moore is in a position to assert the truth of the first proposition, namely that good is simple and indefinable. The next step in the argument of the book is to illustrate the mistakes into which moral philosophers have been led by overlooking this, and thereby committing the naturalistic fallacy. Rather confusingly, Moore divides those theories of the nature of good which commit the fallacy into two groups, the naturalistic and the metaphysical. Both types of theory suggest that there is some definition or analysis of good to be found, but the first kind seeks to define good in terms of some natural object, the second in terms of a metaphysical object. This is the distinction Moore makes. Unfortunately it is not only obscure in itself, but it is also additionally confusing in the light of the fact that the fallacy which both types of theory equally are supposed to commit is the *naturalistic* fallacy. However, once again, if Moore's terminology is less than perfect, this need not unduly alarm us.

The first kind of theory Moore considers is naturalism proper, and he takes as his examples first the evolutionary theory of Spencer, according to which 'good' means 'more evolved'; and secondly the hedonistic utilitarianism of, among others, John Stuart Mill. It will be enough to examine his criticism of the last of these, to get more light on what exactly is supposed by Moore to be so bad about naturalism.

Introducing his criticism, Moore says (p. 59)

. . . that pleasure has been so generally held to be the sole good, is almost entirely due to the fact that it has seemed to be somehow involved in the *definition* of good . . . to be pointed out by the very meaning of the word. If this is so, then the prevalence of Hedonism has been mainly due to what I have called the naturalistic fallacy— the failure to distinguish clearly that unique and indefinable quality which we mean by good.

Moore quotes Mill's words in order to establish, in the first place, that he uses the expressions 'good as an end' and 'desirable as an end' as absolutely equivalent expressions. He then suggests that Mill tries to prove that pleasure is the only thing desirable as an end by appeal to the fact that people do actually desire it and it alone as an end. This attempted proof is, he says, a glaring example of the naturalistic fallacy. Mill's proof consists in arguing that 'desirable' is like 'visible'; and just as you could establish what things were visible by finding out what things people actually saw, so you could find out what things were desirable by discovering what people actually desired. What they do desire, Mill says, is pleasure, and therefore pleasure is desirable and therefore it is good; and since pleasure is *all* that people desire, it can be said not only to be good, but to be *the* good. Moore's criticism of Mill's argument here has had a considerable effect upon the subsequent history of ethics, and therefore it is worth considering both what Mill's argument was in fact meant to show, and what precisely it was of which Moore accused him.

Mill started by saying that it is impossible to prove the truth of statements about ultimate ends. 'Whatever can be proved to be good, must be so by being shown to be a means to something admitted to be good without proof.' With this of course Moore does not disagree; for Mill is simply making the distinction which it is the purpose of Moore's book to establish, between the type of ethical statement for which evidence is required and the type for which there can be no evidence. But Mill goes on, just as Moore does, to attempt to show what things are as a matter of fact good as ends. His argument here, as we have seen, falls into two parts: first he argues that pleasure or happiness is good as an end, and secondly, more dubiously, that it is the only thing which is good as an end. Now though Moore admits that he agrees with Mill's initial distinction between propositions which are and those which are not susceptible of proof, he does not, I think, realize that his approval of Mill ought to go further. When Mill uses the argument from the analogy between 'visible' and 'desirable' he is attempting to establish what things are good, and this, Moore constantly assures us, is a perfectly legitimate undertaking. Mill is not, that is to say, going back on his contention that it is impossible to *prove* what is good as an end. He is saying rather that if people did not already regard some things as ends, and therefore desire them, it would be impossible to prove to them that these things really were ends. 'How is it possible to prove,' he asks, 'that health is good?' The answer is that it is *not* possible to prove it; but the fact is that everybody knows that it is good, and shows this by desiring it. When he says 'the sole evidence it is possible to produce that anything is desirable, is that people actually do desire it' he is repeating the same point. 'The sole evidence' is not evidence in the sense of *proof* that something is good, but it is evidence simply that people already know, without waiting for proof, that it is good. In the very next sentence, Mill makes this clear: 'If the end which the utilitarian doctrine proposes to itself were not, in theory and practice, acknowledged to be an end, nothing could ever convince any person that it was so.' The question of proving what is an ultimate end does not arise; but you can find out what people recognize as ultimate ends by finding out what they desire. What they desire, Mill goes on to say, is happiness. I cannot see anything wrong or fallacious about this. But Moore's criticism of this first part of Mill's argument has become part of the accepted dogma of moral philosophy. This has been due partly to misunderstanding Mill, in the way that Moore taught us to, but partly also to misunderstanding Moore. That Moore did misunderstand Mill is fairly clear. Mill, he said, committed the naturalistic fallacy because he defined 'good' which is indefinable; and he committed it in its strongest form, because he identified good, which is non-natural, with a natural thing, namely 'what is desired'. Moore does not object to Mill's identification of 'good' with 'desirable'. This is at first sight surprising, for we have come to expect that the identification of good with anything would count as a commission of the fallacy. But the reason is that, according to Moore, 'desirable' means 'worthy to be desired'; and 'worthy to be desired' must mean 'good'; therefore the identification of 'good' with 'desirable' does not matter, in the sense that it is actually tautological. Moore does not actually say this in so many words, but it is assumed in his argument. His attack is levelled against the passage from the concept of desirability to that of being desired. 'The fallacy,' he says (p. 67), 'in this step is so obvious that it is quite wonderful how Mill failed to see it.' There is, after all, he claims, no analogy between 'visible' and 'desirable'. 'Visible' means 'able to be seen', but 'desirable' does not mean 'able to be desired' but 'fit to be desired'. The analogy is rather to be sought between 'desirable' and 'damnable', which does not mean what *is*

damned, but what should be damned. It is this part of Moore's
argument which appears to have fascinated moral philosophers
and from which they have drawn such inspiration that it has
sometimes seemed as if there were no other virtue in a moral
philosopher except that he should avoid the naturalistic fallacy.
But, in the first place, as an argument against Mill it is misconceived. If Mill had first defined 'good' as 'desirable' and had
then gone on to define 'desirable' as 'desired', he would no
doubt have been open to criticism. But it was no part of his
interest to define 'good' or 'desirable' at all. Indeed, if anything,
his remarks about the impossibility of proving propositions concerned with ultimate ends would suggest that he agreed with
Moore that 'good' was indefinable, though it need not mean this.
The fact is that the question of definition was never raised by
him at all. He was interested in discovering the underlying
principles of ethical conduct, and not in defining ethical terms.
His introduction of the concept of 'what is desired' was, as I
hope I have shown, due to the very fact that you cannot prove
what is or is not good. All that you have to go on is what people
think is good, what, that is, they have always thought worth
desiring. What they have always thought worth desiring is what
they have in fact desired. Mill's procedure here is like Hume's,
who argues that the qualities which we have come to regard as
virtuous are those which we in fact find are desired for the sake
of the general well-being of society; and it is not so very unlike
Moore's own procedure when, in the last chapter of *Principia
Ethica*, he turns to consider the question what things are intrinsically good. In each case the question at issue is: What is it
that people value most highly? Mill's perhaps unduly simple
answer is, happiness, Mill cannot, therefore, be rightly accused
of trying to define 'good'; and this accusation must be at least
part of what Moore meant by his statement that the naturalistic
fallacy had been committed, since we have been told over and
over again that the naturalistic fallacy consists in just this. But,
even if Mill had been trying to define 'good', and had therefore
offered 'what is desired' as a definition of 'desirable', which he
did not, I think that Moore would have been unduly hard on
him. If the argument comes down to a discussion of the meanings of words, then, though the analogy between the meanings

N.B. ||

||

*Moore distinguishes 'the Good' from 'good things'. There is nothing wrong
with defining or giving examples of the latter, or even with saying
that one thing only is good. What Moore objects to is defining the
Good. Thus, for him the nat. fal. consists in confusing the Good
with good things — the goodness of a thing with the thing. The
problem consists precisely in his assumption, as W. brings out, that*

of 'desirable' and 'visible' is not close, still the distinction between 'desired' and 'desirable' is not so clear and sharp as Moore suggests. When house agents speak of houses as desirable they do not mean that these houses are such that we ought to desire them. Very often 'desirable' means something like 'what any sane person would desire', and if this is what it means, then the relevance of the consideration of what sane people do in fact desire is at once obvious. But this defence of Mill should not be taken very seriously, for I hope I have said enough to show why I do not believe that for Mill the question was one of the meanings of words at all.

I said just now that not only Mill but Moore also was misrepresented by those moral philosophers who attached great importance to the breakdown of the analogy between 'visible' and 'desirable'. I do not mean to suggest that Moore himself did not think it important. I am sure that he did; and in this particular chapter of *Principia Ethica* there is no doubt that the major fault of the utilitarians is taken to be that they defined 'good', which is a non-natural property, in terms of pleasure or desire, which are natural objects. For instance, twice in this chapter Moore sums up his arguments against the first part of Mill's contention, namely the contention that pleasure or happiness is desirable. The first summary is as follows (p. 73):

In this argument, the naturalistic fallacy is plainly involved. That fallacy, I explained, consists in the contention that good means nothing but some simple or complex notion, that can be defined in terms of natural qualities. In Mill's case, good is thus supposed to *mean* simply what is desired; and what is desired is something which can thus be defined in natural terms. Mill tells us that we ought to desire something (an ethical proposition) because we actually do desire it; but if his contention that 'I ought to desire' means nothing but 'I do desire' were true, then he is only entitled to say, 'we do desire so and so because we do desire it'; and that is not an ethical proposition at all; it is a mere tautology.

It is to be noticed that in this summary he uses the argument against defining 'good' which he used in the first chapter, namely that if you do define it, you are landed with a tautology; and this has nothing specially to do with the naturalism or otherwise of the terms of the definition. There is here, in fact, the very same ambiguity which was to be found in the first chapter, where Moore called his fallacy 'naturalistic' but went on to say that the metaphysical philosophers who defined 'good' in terms of non-natural objects committed the fallacy just as much as the naturalists did. Once again, he is first and foremost accusing Mill of attempting to define good, and secondarily accusing him of naturalism, in the ordinary sense . . . that is of reducing non-natural to natural concepts. Moore's second summary (p. 108) at the very end of the chapter is shorter. There he simply states that his refutation of utilitarianism consists, in the first part, in pointing out that Mill commits the naturalistic fallacy 'in identifying "desirable" with "desired"'. Now it is very easy to read this as meaning that the whole of the fallacy consists in passing from the non-natural concept 'desirable' to the natural concept 'desired'. And this is how later philosophers have been inclined to regard it, though they have usually substituted the more specific and understandable expression 'ethical' for 'non-natural', and 'non-ethical' for 'natural'. But even here it is important to remember that at least part of what Moore was attacking was the identifying of 'desirable' with anything at all, on the grounds that 'desirable' was somehow identical with 'good'. Even if, in this particular chapter, Moore was chiefly concerned with naturalism properly so called, nevertheless, regarding the book as a whole, it must be admitted that the simplicity and unanalysability of the quality of goodness was his major concern, and it was as overlooking *this* that his fallacy was chiefly supposed to be fallacious.

In connexion with this same argument of Mill's, there is a further difficulty in Moore's treatment, which may perhaps be thought to be fundamental, and that is the difficulty of understanding exactly what Moore meant by 'natural' and 'non-natural'. It might be held with some plausibility that if this point is not clear, then no part of the argument which is concerned with the naturalistic fallacy can be clear either. But in fact I do not think this would be fair, for two reasons. The first I have laboured enough already, and that is that I do not believe the distinction between natural and non-natural was as important for Moore's purposes as the title of his fallacy would suggest. The second reason is that it is fairly clear from the

examples that he gives what *kinds* of thing he means to characterize as natural and non-natural objects, although it is obscure
why he talks of *objects*; and he also fails actually to provide any
satisfactory definition, in *Principia Ethica* itself. Later, he was
apparently willing to accept a criterion for 'non-natural' which
suggested that a non-natural property was one which could not
be discerned by the senses.[1] This, in its turn, is exceedingly
obscure; but this and Moore's own use suggest that at any rate
metaphysical concepts such as 'more real' and ethical concepts
such as 'good' would be non-natural because non-sensory; while
yellowness or pleasantness would be natural, because detected
by the senses. But I think that those philosophers who have
attempted to state the doctrine of *Principia Ethica* in terms
merely of ethical as contrasted with non-ethical terms, have
misrepresented Moore. They have somehow put the cart before
the horse. Moore, when he laid down that non-natural properties
could not be defined in terms of natural properties, conceived
himself to be making a perfectly general point, from which, in
conjunction with the premise that 'good' was the name of a
simple property, it could be inferred that 'good' could not be
analysed at all. If 'non-natural' simply meant 'ethical', then one
part of this inference would go. For since nobody would dispute
that 'good' was, or could be, an ethical term, to say 'good' is non-
natural and therefore cannot be defined in natural terms would,
on this interpretation, be to state only that 'good' cannot be
defined in non-ethical terms, not to *derive* this from any more
general prohibition. This would reduce the interest, though
perhaps it would not affect the truth of Moore's position.

So far I have discussed only Moore's treatment of the first
part of the utilitarian argument and this is by far the most
important part of his criticism. But Mill had not only to establish that pleasure or happiness was desirable in itself, but also
that it was the *only* thing desirable in itself. Mill admits that
whether or not this second proposition is true is a psychological

[1] See *The Philosophy of G. E. Moore*: The Library of Living Philosophers, editor Paul Arthur Schilpp (North-western University,
Evanston, Illinois, 1942); C. D. Broad, 'Certain Features in Moore's
Ethical Doctrines', pp. 43 *sqq.*; and G. E. Moore, 'Reply to my Critics',
pp. 581 *sqq.*

matter, and therefore his answer is supposed to be based on empirical evidence. But he concludes by saying that 'to desire anything except in proportion as the idea of it is pleasant, is a physical and metaphysical impossibility'. This is rather mysterious. 'Metaphysical impossibility' suggests that it is supposed to be necessarily true that we desire only pleasure. But if this is so, it is hard to see how the question whether we do or not could be said to be one of psychology. The trouble arises largely, it seems to me, because of the extreme difficulty of using expressions such as 'pleasure' or 'for the sake of pleasure' intelligibly. There is in fact no contradiction between saying that we desire something for its own sake and that we desire it for the sake of pleasure, in at least one possible meaning of that expression. Moore is very savage with Mill for saying just this.

Pray consider a moment [he says (p. 72)] what this contemptible nonsense really means. 'Money,' says Mill, 'is only desired as a means to happiness.' Perhaps so, but what then? 'Why,' says Mill, 'money is undoubtedly desired for its own sake.' 'Yes, go on,' say we. 'Well,' says Mill, 'if money is desired for its own sake, it must be desirable as an end-in-itself: I have said so myself.' 'Oh,' say we, 'but you also just now said that it was only desirable as a means.' 'I own I did,' says Mill, 'but I will try to patch up matters, by saying that what is only a means to an end is the same thing as a part of that end. I daresay the public won't notice.' And the public haven't noticed.

Once again, I feel inclined to defend Mill. The language of means and ends would doubtless be better dropped, since it does suggest just the incompatibility which Moore finds. But there is no need to employ it. If Mill had instead talked about doing things 'for the sake of pleasure or happiness' and 'for their own sake' then I should find nothing ludicrous in his remarks. This, then, is one part of Moore's criticism of Mill's argument to show that only pleasure is desired. He argues that Mill confuses what is a means to an end with what is part of an end. I do not think this criticism is well founded. On the other hand, it is because one can speak of pleasure in these ways that it can be made to look plausible to say we desire nothing except pleasure. For whatever end anybody suggests as a possible object of desire it is always open to Mill to say that pleasure is part of that end, though the end *is* desired for its own sake. And because it is open to him in every case whatever to do this, he is really landed with an uninteresting tautology. Pleasure turns out to be 'whatever we desire', and therefore, necessarily, whatever we desire turns out to be pleasure. This necessity, which is the necessity of tautology, is, I suspect, what Mill was referring to, confusingly, as the *metaphysical* impossibility of desiring anything but pleasure.

The second part of Moore's criticism is borrowed from Bradley. Mill confuses, says Moore (p. 74), 'a pleasant thought' with 'the thought of a pleasure'. It is only where the thought of a pleasure is present that the pleasure can be said to be the object of desire or the motive to action. Where there is only, for instance, the pleasant thought that I will have a drink, I do not have the drink for the sake of the pleasure, but for the sake of the drink. The pleasant thought is here, Moore says, the cause of my action, but not the motive, and therefore pleasure is not the object of my desire. This objection is ingenious, and there is no doubt a distinction here to be made. But even this is not enough to prevent Mill using the word pleasure if he chooses to do so as 'the object of all desire'.

I am aware that this discussion of pleasure is highly unsatisfactory. I do not think that either Mill or Moore was entirely clear what sort of a problem they had before them. The only excuse for treating it so cursorily is that Moore's criticism of this second part of Mill's argument is of comparatively little importance whether regarded as a part of Moore's own ethical theory, or as a factor in the subsequent history of the subject. On the other hand his criticism of the first part, his allegation that Mill has committed the naturalistic fallacy, is, as I have said, of very great importance, and to later philosophers' interpretations of this we shall have cause to return.

Having shown how Spencer and the utilitarians committed the naturalistic fallacy by attempting to define 'good' in empirical terms, Moore in the next chapter goes on to show how the same fallacy was committed by those philosophers who tried to explain the nature of goodness in a quite different way, namely by reference to metaphysics. We have seen how these metaphysical philosophers thought that they were reinstating ethics by divorcing it from naturalism. Moore thought, on the

other hand, that their treatment of the subject was no less fatal
and destructive than that of the empiricists. He gave them
credit, it is true, for realizing the possibility of the existence of
properties other than natural properties; or rather for recogniz-
ing, as he says, that there may be objects of knowledge which
do not exist in time, and which we do not perceive. But he
criticized them for supposing that these possible objects of
knowledge were actually existing, though super-sensible objects. At this point it is very difficult to be clear exactly what
the difference between Moore and the metaphysicians was.
For Moore himself, in the first chapter of *Principia Ethica*, insisted, as he insists throughout the book, that 'good' is the name
of a supersensible property of things. What he apparently does
not want to say is that goodness *exists*. He maintains that metaphysical philosophers have been led on to the absurdity of saying that goodness exists by a false analogy between ordinary
empirical propositions, such as that I am writing, and propositions of the form 'This is good' (pp. 111 *sqq.*). Empirical
propositions, Moore says, do assert a relation between two or
more *existent* things, and metaphysicians are unable to believe
that you can ever assert a proposition without asserting that
something or other exists. Moore thinks that, to take a non-
ethical example, when you assert that $2 + 2 = 4$, what you
mean is 'merely what you say' and you do not mean that 2 and
4 exist, nor that anything else exists at all. 'Every truth, they
[the metaphysicians] think, must mean somehow that something exists; and since, unlike the empiricists, they recognize
some truths which do not mean that anything exists here and
now, these they think must mean that something exists *not* here
and now.' So far this is intelligible enough. But when Moore
goes on to apply this to the particular case of ethics it is less
easy to see what he means.

On the same principle, since 'good' is a predicate which neither does
nor can exist, they are bound to suppose either that to be good means
to be related to some other particular thing which can exist and does
exist in reality; or else that it means merely 'to belong to the real
world'—that goodness is transcended or absorbed in reality.

The oddity is to find Moore saying that goodness is a predicate which cannot exist. But what he means is that when you say that something is good, as when you say that $2 + 2 = 4$, you mean merely 'what you say'. No analysis or elucidation of it is possible. No *other* actual or possible object needs to be brought in to explain what it is you are asserting. If asked what you mean, all you could do would be to repeat that you meant the thing was good. Moore does not mean to suggest that there is no such predicate as good, nor that 'good' is not the name of an actual property which things have; only that *what property it is* cannot be explained in terms of a super-sensible 'reality' over and above what we see, any more than it can be explained in terms of what we do see. His use of 'existing' is perhaps muddling. He appears to use it to mean existing in either of two ways, namely 'in time', which is how empirical objects exist, or 'not in time', which is how the supposed total and unified reality of the metaphysicians is held to exist. Since he does not want to say that the property of goodness exists in either of these ways, he suggests that it does not exist at all; and this, on the ordinary interpretation of 'exists', is contrary to his own stated views.

Moore maintains that it is mistaken to suppose any connexion between metaphysics and ethics. The main question in ethics being, as he said in the first chapter, the nature of goodness, no investigations of the general features of reality can possibly throw any light on this. To hope that one could explain goodness in terms of reality in general, must be to commit the naturalistic fallacy, for it must imply that goodness is *not*, as in fact it is, unanalysable in terms of anything else. The simple nature of goodness is not to be explained by any account of the universe as a whole. Moore concedes that it is possible that metaphysics might have some relevance to the question of what we ought to do, though it can have none to the question of what is good. For what we ought to do is determined by some practical and causal questions about the consequences of our acts. Metaphysics, Moore suggests (p. 117), might throw light on what the consequences of our acts will in fact be, though it cannot settle whether or not these consequences will be good. There is a good deal of irony in this apparent concession to the metaphysicians. First, it is not likely that they would happily accept the role of mere practical guides; secondly, the only two examples Moore gives of the way in which metaphysicians could help are not very encouraging. He suggests, in the first place, that if they could definitely prove that there was a system of rewards and punishments after death, this would affect our actions; or alternatively, if they could prove what they do in fact maintain, namely that there is an absolutely unchanging, timelessly real system of which we are part, that time and change are mere illusions, then it would follow that there was no point in action at all (for if reality is unchanging what difference can it make if we act?). This could be said to affect our actions, by showing that all actions were either impossible or unnecessary. The concession, then, that metaphysics could, even in this sense, be relevant to ethics is more apparent than real.

The beliefs of metaphysical philosophers, once they have committed the initial mistake of supposing that their general theories will explain ethics as well, are divided by Moore according to whether they rest on logical or epistemological errors. In the first class he places all those philosophers who hold that moral judgements are like natural laws, and state a necessary connexion between subject and predicate. He associates this mistake with the mistake of supposing that goodness can be explained in terms of a super-sensible reality. For he says such philosophers think of the proposition 'This is good' as stating a relation between two existent entities, but because the predicate is peculiar in being part of unchanging reality, therefore it is connected with its subject in a particularly unchanging way. The metaphysicians and the naturalists proper misconceive the nature of the predicate 'good' in basically the same way. Moore's own manner of talking about predicates and properties is exceedingly surprising (p. 124):

It is immediately obvious that when we see a thing to be good, its goodness is not a property which we can take up in our hands.

But I would challenge anyone to name a property which we *could* take up in our hands, precisely,

or separate from it even by the most delicate scientific instruments, and transfer to something else. . . . But philosophers suppose that the reason why we cannot take goodness up and move it about is not

that it is a different *kind* of object from any which can be moved
about, but only that it *necessarily* exists together with anything with
which it does exist. They explain the type of ethical truths by supposing it identical with the type of scientific law. It is only when
they have done this that the naturalistic philosophers proper—those
who are empiricists—and those whom I have called metaphysical
part company.

The metaphysicians think that there is some absolute necessity
in the laws, derivable from the nature of the universe, while the
naturalists do not. A variation of this logical error is to hold that
the proposition 'This is good' is not a natural law, but some
kind of absolute natural command.

The metaphysical philosophers who, in Moore's view, base
their theories on epistemological rather than logical errors are
those, headed by Kant, who hold that a thing is good if it is
willed in a certain way. Besides Kant, the post-Hegelian English metaphysicians are here the target. Moore calls attention
to the analogy, which, as we saw, was explicitly drawn by
Bradley, between knowing something and bringing it about in
practice. It is equally false, Moore says, to say that if you
understand something in some particular way then you have
understood something true, as it is to say that if you will something in a particular way, then you have willed something good.
That a proposition is true is distinct from the fact that anyone
thinks it true, and that an action is good is distinct from the fact
that anybody wills it, or brings it about. For Bradley, as for
Spinoza, the concept of truth was dependent upon the concept
of understanding. The truth about the universe was identical
with what was understood about the universe. In the same way,
there could be no concept of morally good actions if there were
not already the concept of persons realizing themselves in
action. Truth and goodness are, on this view, both of them
relative. It is only that some acts of will realize the self more
successfully than others. Once again Moore accuses philosophers such as Bradley of failure to see that goodness is a
simple property of things; at the very most, he says, that an
action should have been willed in a certain way could be a test
or criterion of its goodness. It could never be what its goodness
actually consisted in, any more than the truth of a statement

could actually *consist in* its being consistent with other statements, though this might be a test of its truth.

Metaphysical philosophers, then, stand convicted of the naturalistic fallacy. So far are they from reinstating ethics, after the ravages upon it of the utilitarians, that they actually make matters worse, for the non-naturalism of their version of the fallacy might deceive people into thinking that no fallacy had been committed. Moore's treatment of the metaphysical moral philosophers is a particularly good example of the extreme and marvellous literalness of his mind. He represents metaphysicians as just asserting that a number of extraordinary objects, such as the true self, or the real will, exist; and as simply asserting that goodness is to be analysed in terms of such objects. Of course they do assert these things, but not perhaps quite in the manner which Moore suggests. If anyone started to expound a metaphysical system in Moore's language, or Moore's tone of voice, he would not, it is true, win much acceptance for his theory. But what Moore in no way allows for, and it may be thought rightly, is the very different tone of voice of these philosophers themselves. Moore makes no concessions to the satisfaction which is to be gained from the contemplation of a highly general theory, from which truths about human conduct are to be deduced, as a mere part of the whole. This is the kind of satisfaction which is to be got from reading Spinoza, in whose system human passions and human behaviour are fitted into the general scheme, and propositions about them are supposedly deduced with the rigour of Euclid from propositions about the nature of substance. It would be useless, as a means of giving this particular kind of pleasure, to invent a system, the point of which was exclusively to account for human obligations and which, in order to do this, considered nothing but human nature. The metaphysical pleasure precisely consists in *not* being the centre of the universe, but in seeing familiar problems, such as the problem of how it is right to behave, somehow reduced, and also answered, by being shown to be part of a total scheme of things. This kind of pleasure may be partially aesthetic; it certainly has very little to do with how many of the propositions contained in the system are actually true statements. Moore, judging other philosophers by his own standards, tends to speak of the metaphysicians as though they had intended to set out a series of true statements of fact—that this, that or the other object existed; because of this his discussions of their writings seem sometimes rather odd, and unlike what they actually wrote. But he is surely right in saying that they, all of them, attempted to derive ethics from something non-ethical. If this is the naturalistic fallacy, then they committed it; and their committing it is the secret both of their charm and of their power.

We are now at last in a position to consider Moore's own positive contribution to ethics. This is to be found mainly in the last two chapters of *Principia Ethica*. These two chapters have had very little influence indeed upon the subsequent course of moral philosophy; it is, however, worth remarking that Moore has perhaps been more frequently misrepresented than most other moral philosophers, and this is largely due to the neglect of these two chapters. Chapter Five of *Principia Ethica* is entitled 'Ethics in relation to Conduct'. At the beginning of it, Moore summarizes the course of the argument so far (p. 142). He has first, he says, tried to show what the adjective 'good' means; he has then discussed various proposed self-evident principles of ethics. The conclusion of this second step was negative, namely that neither pleasure nor any non-natural object was the sole good. The final step in the argument of the book is to deal positively with the question, What things are good? But this final step is postponed till the last chapter. In the present chapter he declares his intention of dealing with a quite separate question, namely What ought we to do? It will be seen therefore, that on Moore's own admission, this chapter is outside the main course of the argument, and it is fairly clear that he is far less interested in this question about conduct than in the more general question about what is good. His theory of conduct is extremely simple. There is no such thing as a moral obligation which is not an obligation to produce the greatest amount of good. 'Our "duty", therefore, can only be defined as that action which will cause more good to exist in the universe than any possible alternative.' What we ought to do is always, he thinks, to be determined by a calculation of the consequences of our act, and an assessment of the goodness or badness of these. Thus, on the question of conduct, Moore is in far closer agreement with the utilitarians than with any other moral philosophers. The utilitarians held that an act was to be regarded as a duty if its consequences were such as to produce greater total happiness than misery. Moore held that an act was a duty if it produced more good than harm. They differ only about the question of how to assess the value of the consequences. On the question of general moral rules, too, Moore is in close agreement with Hume, Austin, and Mill. The utilitarians, on the whole, held that established moral rules, such as the rule not to commit murder, must be regarded as universally binding for two reasons: first because the wisdom of past generations has discovered that the consequences of murder are in fact conducive to misery rather than happiness; secondly because even in the case of an apparent exception, where the murder might seem certain to have good consequences, still the rule should be kept, because in general it is right, and one breach of it has, among other things, the consequence of weakening the authority of the rule, which we wish to see generally observed. But Mill does not deny the possibility that sometimes these general moral principles may conflict with each other, or may seem inadequate to the complexities of the situation, and in this case a direct consideration of the particular contemplated action, without reference to general principles, may be necessary, and an attempt must be made to assess the consequences of this individual act. In general, Moore is in complete agreement with this view. But he states more clearly than any utilitarian that there can be no certainty attaching to moral rules. Since moral rules lay down duties, and since duties are determined by consequences, they can never be more than probably right, since certainty about the consequences of actions is impossible. But in the case of fairly broad *types* of action, such as lying, stealing, or murder, the probability that the consequences will be harmful are fairly high, and Moore would subscribe to the two reasons given by the utilitarians for not breaking these general, well-worn moral rules. But he is far more explicit than Mill in allowing that there may be a great number of cases in which the only moral rule which would apply would be a new or revolutionary rule, or where, owing to the complexity and particularity of the circumstances, no rule can be formulated at all. In such cases, Moore says, 'The individual should rather guide his choice by a direct consideration of the intrinsic value or vileness of the effects which his action may produce.' Such considerations as this can, he says, lead to definite and certain conclusions. That is, you may be able positively to assert that if you do a certain action, and if the consequences which will probably follow from it do in fact follow from it, then you will have produced good rather than harm. In this case you must perform the act, if you wish to do what is right. There is still an element of probability in your assertion, namely the probability that the consequences will be as you predict; but there is also, Moore says, the certainty, if you give your mind to discovering it, of the intrinsic worth of the consequences. Moral rules, then, are basically predictions about what will happen. They may therefore always be falsified. Sometimes where there is no stock moral rule to help us, we have to make our own predictions and assessments, and in these cases we do not and cannot attempt to generalize. Each case is decided on its own facts. This theory seems to me to have extreme beauty and economy, and to fit many of the facts of moral life. It succeeds as few other moral theories, except Hume's, do, in allowing for the difference between those cases where the possession of a principle, the avoidance of breaking a rule, is the paramount consideration (as, for instance, where we feel we must keep a promise, because there is a principle against breaking promises); and those cases where we feel it would be immoral to be bound by any ready-made principle, since none would be adequate to the situation. We may not share Moore's confidence that it is possible to see, if we attend to the matter, what has the property of goodness and what has not; but that we try to work out in some such way what it is right to do seems to me beyond question.

Finally, in the last chapter, Moore addresses himself to the question what things in fact possess intrinsic goodness. The method which must be employed, he says, to decide what things have intrinsic value and in what degree, is to consider what things are such that if they existed by themselves in absolute isolation we should yet judge their existence to be good; and to settle the question of degrees of value we must compare these isolated things. This, so far, might not seem to give us much help; and we feel obstinately inclined to ask how we could know when we had come across something with intrinsic value, let alone how we should know if we had carried out the comparison rightly. For Moore, however, there suddenly seem to be no difficulties left (p. 188).

Once the meaning of the question is clearly understood, the answer to it, in its main outlines, appears to be so obvious, that it runs the risk of seeming to be a platitude. By far the most valuable things, which we know or can imagine, are certain states of consciousness which may be roughly described as the pleasures of human inter-course and the enjoyment of beautiful objects. No one probably, who has asked himself the question, has ever doubted that personal affection and the appreciation of what is beautiful in Art or Nature, are good in themselves; nor if we consider strictly what things are worth having *purely for their own sakes*, does it appear probable that any one will think anything else has *nearly* so great a value as the things which are included under these two heads.

The rest of the chapter is devoted to a further analysis of these intrinsically good things, and a discussion of what things are intrinsically bad. The great evils are three in kind: the love of what is ugly or bad; the hatred of what is beautiful or good; and the consciousness of pain. Moore is aware that his con-clusions in this chapter may *seem* arbitrary; but since they seem to him obviously true, there is no serious sense in which he can agree that they are arbitrary. He does, however, agree that they are not particularly systematic or unified. But this, he thinks, is just the nature of the case.

To search for 'unity' and 'system' at the expense of truth is not, I take it, the proper business of philosophy, however universally it may have been the practice of philosophers. And that all truths about the universe possess to one another all the various relations which may be meant by 'unity' can only be legitimately asserted when we have carefully distinguished those various relations and discovered what those truths are.

The only two questions which should be asked, he concludes, of any object of ethical inquiry, are first, Has it intrinsic value?

and second, Is it a means to the best possible? The results of his attempt to reduce the legitimate questions of ethics to these two will, he says, surprise philosophers but he hopes that they will be acceptable to common sense.

Brief quotation from this final chapter of *Principia Ethica* cannot convey the impression of force and passion which strikes one as one reads it. But if philosophers were, as Moore predicted, surprised by it, they hid their surprise in total silence—perhaps the silence of embarrassment. Moore has frequently been spoken of as the philosopher who concentrated our attention upon the meaning of the word 'good'; and who exposed most fully the nature of the naturalistic fallacy in ethics. This second feat was a matter, it is generally agreed, of great importance, although it is also agreed that the fallacy itself, and arguments against it, had occupied the attention of English moral philosophers from the seventeenth century. I do not of course want to dispute either of these claims to fame. But I think that Moore's concentration on the meaning of the word 'good' should be considered side by side with his insistence that the point of ethics was to state what things are good; and his exposure of the naturalistic fallacy should be considered in the context of his claim that 'good' is the name of a simple un-analysable quality of things. Moore was not primarily concerned to discuss the nature of moral words, nor to analyse what does and does not constitute, in general, an ethical argument. His concern was simply to find out what things were good and what were bad. Not surprisingly, therefore, though the final chapter of his book was neglected by philosophers, it had a powerful effect upon people actually interested in answering these questions. This effect was, it must be admitted, partly produced, not so much by Moore's actual arguments, as by his personality; but I think there is no passage in all his writing which conveys so powerful an impression of personality as this. Keynes, in his memoir 'My Early Beliefs',[1] has much that is extremely sympathetic and extremely funny to say about the effect which Moore had upon himself and his contemporaries at Cambridge. He quotes from the last chapter of *Principia*

[1] J. M. Keynes, *Two Memoirs*, p. 94; Rupert Hart-Davis, London, 1949.

Ethica, the chapter which he considered contained Moore's religion; and he wrote of it as follows:

The New Testament is a handbook for politicians compared with the unworldliness of Moore's chapter on the Ideal. I know no equal to it in literature since Plato. And it is better than Plato because it is quite free from *fancy.* It conveys the beauty of the literalness of Moore's mind, the pure and passionate intensity of his vision, *un*fanciful and *un*dressed up. Moore had a nightmare once in which he could not distinguish propositions from tables. But even when awake, he could not distinguish love and beauty and truth from the furniture. They took on the same definition of outline, the same stable, solid objective qualities and common sense reality. I see no reason [Keynes goes on] to shift from the fundamental intuitions of *Principia Ethica*; though they are much too few and too narrow to fit actual experience. That they furnish a justification of experience wholly independent of outside events has become an added comfort, even though one cannot live today secure in the undisturbed individualism which was the extraordinary achievement of the early Edwardian days.

3
Intuitionism

AFTER THE PUBLICATION of *Principia Ethica*, the climate, in England, was on the whole unfavourable to metaphysical speculation in ethics. It was not so much Moore's actual arguments against the metaphysicians as his whole method of writing, on this and other subjects, which seemed to demand that in future philosophy must be written carefully, and attention must be paid to the actual literal meaning of what was said. I propose to consider next a group of writers, who, like Moore, were, broadly speaking, intuitionists, and who, like him, renounced all claim to deduce an ethical theory from any wide explanatory theory of the nature of reality at large. Typical of this group were the Oxford philosophers Carritt, Prichard, Ross, and Joseph, and in Cambridge, C. D. Broad. I cannot discuss all their theories in detail, but by considering the work of two of them, Prichard and Ross, I hope to be able to show what kinds of methods were used, and conclusions reached. Prichard's publications on moral philosophy were in the form of various articles and lectures, which have now been collected and published together in a book entitled *Moral Obligation*. In his writings, intuitionism can be seen in perhaps its most extreme form; and since his appeal in making his points is seldom to reason but usually to 'what will seem obvious if the reader thinks clearly for a moment'; since, that is, we are required to follow arguments less often than to make admissions of what we are supposed really to think, to summarize his views is a matter of some difficulty. The result will inevitably seem somewhat random.

Perhaps the most famous of Prichard's articles was one published in *Mind* in 1912, entitled 'Does Moral Philosophy Rest on a Mistake?'[1] The main purpose of this article was to suggest that arguments are out of place in trying to settle the question of what obligations we are under; and therefore that moral philosophy as hitherto conceived is a non-existent subject. This is of course an exaggeration; but it does appear that Prichard thought of himself as pioneering to introduce a new version of the subject, with new clarity of method and new accuracy. One of the most surprising things about the opening paragraphs of this article is his apparent unawareness of the existence of similar arguments both in Bradley and in Moore. 'Personally,' he says, 'I have been led by growing dissatisfaction . . . to wonder whether the subject . . . consists in an attempt to answer an improper question.' The improper question is supposed to be the demand for reasons why something which has the characteristic of being obligatory, has this characteristic. All demands, he says, for proof that something is a duty are mistaken. This view is related to Bradley's. For Bradley explicitly stated that in his opinion the question Why should I be moral? was nonsensical both in general, and in particular cases. But the likeness to Moore is of course far greater. For Moore's main purpose was, as we have seen, precisely to distinguish those statements in morals for which proof could be given from those for which it could not. And though he, in *Principia Ethica* at least, confined his attention to the characteristic of goodness, and said that statements which ascribed goodness to anything were such that proof was impossible, while Prichard's main concern is with the obligatory, still the likeness is considerable; and indeed in his later book, *Ethics*, Moore also was inclined to treat 'obligatoriness' as another intuitable property. Neither Prichard nor Ross seemed to notice any particular debt to Moore. There are few references to him in Prichard's book, and nearly all that there are are derogatory. He came off a little better at the hands of Ross, who is very careful and fair in his discussions of other philosophers. But neither showed any awareness of the closeness, in many essentials, of their own work to his. But perhaps it is naïve to be surprised at this. Even when considering books

[1] *Moral Obligation*, pp. 1 *sqq.*

written less than half a century ago, it is absurdly easy to regard
them as forming a continuous stream of publication, in which
the later works somehow flow out of those which came before.
We tend to regard Moore as the source, because of the historical
accident that *Principia Ethica* was published at the beginning
of the century, and because of the powerful impression that he
makes upon us. It is difficult not to think, not only of the later
as flowing from the earlier, but of the lesser as at least influenced
by the greater. But perhaps even 'influence' is too strong a word
to use. In any case, if we were to pursue the sources of intuitionism, we should have to go back at least as far as Sidgwick,
which would be beyond the scope of this book. The impression
remains, however, that Prichard's article was not quite so
revolutionary as its title suggests.

I return now to the article itself. Answers to the question
'Why should we do our duty?' take, he says, one of two forms.
Either they say that doing it would be for our happiness, or
alternatively that doing it realizes some good. In the strongest
cases these two views are combined, and it is suggested that
happiness is the good to be realized. But, Prichard says, there
is a gap between the concept of 'good' and the concept of 'what
I ought to bring about'. It is always possible, when you have
accepted somebody's argument that a thing is good, to go on
to ask 'But why should I bring it about?' Prichard considers
only briefly, in order to reject it, the view that 'good' and 'what
I should bring about' mean the same, or are to be defined one
in terms of the other. In any case that would make no serious
difference to his case. His point is that ultimately the gap between the apprehension that a thing has any characteristic whatever and the apprehension that it is a duty has to remain
unclosed. The apprehension that something is a duty is always
a further step. Moore had defined duty in terms of good, and
then said that the apprehension of goodness was always a
further step, beyond the apprehension of the other qualities of
a thing. In his later book, *Ethics*, he regarded the apprehension
that something was a duty as separate from the apprehension
that it was good, and equally irreducible. Prichard, at least in
this article, is inclined to think that the ultimate quality, which
cannot be analysed, is that of *being a duty*. If goodness is a

rather mysterious quality, obligatoriness seems to me even more so; but I shall return in a moment to the curious difficulties into which Prichard gets, through regarding it as a property of actions. For the moment let us return to this first article. While Bradley appealed to moral consciousness for confirmation of his views, Prichard seems to appeal to something more like common sense. He does not try to show that there is a logical fallacy in identifying obligatoriness with something else; he simply maintains that we do not really do it.

Suppose we ask ourselves whether our sense that we ought to pay our debts or to tell the truth arises from our recognition that in doing so we should be originating something good, e.g. material comfort in A or true belief in B, i.e. suppose we ask ourselves whether it is this aspect of the action which leads to our recognition that we ought to do it. We at once and without hesitation answer 'no'.[1]

Common sense apparently tells us that when we say that something is a duty, or should be done, we are reporting what we simply see to be so.

This apprehension is immediate, in precisely the same sense in which a mathematical apprehension is immediate, e.g. the apprehension that this three-sided figure, in virtue of its being three-sided, must have three angles. Both apprehensions are immediate in the sense that in both, insight into the nature of the subject directly leads us to recognize its possession of the predicate; and it is only stating this fact from the other side to say that in both cases the fact apprehended is self-evident.[2]

It is not clear exactly what is meant by 'self-evident', but the mathematical example seems to show that Prichard regards moral truths as necessary. He certainly regards them as indubitable. There has been, he thinks, a parallel in the history of epistemology to the mistake he is calling attention to in the history of morals, namely an insistence on asking for proofs where none is available. (Like Bradley, he just states the analogy between the theory of knowledge and that of morals; but it is perhaps his nearest approach to an argument.) In epistemology, philosophers such as Descartes have been led, by noticing that

---

[1] *Moral Obligation*, p. 4.   [2] *op. cit.* p. 8.

we all of us sometimes make mistakes, to raise the question whether there can be a proof that, in some cases at least, we are *not* mistaken. Since in any given case, they argue, it is possible to make a mistake, we can never be certain unless we have proof, that in the particular case before us we are not mistaken. Therefore, Prichard says, these philosophers embarked upon a hopeless quest for proof that what we take to be knowledge really is knowledge. But, he says, they have overlooked the fact of the matter, which is that scepticism is impossible. For since when you know something you always and necessarily know also *that* you know it, you cannot be mistaken when you come across something that you know. Genuine knowledge carries with it a kind of trade mark such that it is impossible to mistake it for anything else. If you know, you can't be wrong. Descartes had just failed to notice the trade mark which knowledge carries. In moral theory, then, the same mistake is supposed to occur. The demand for proof of the truth of ultimate moral intuitions is as nonsensical as the demand for proof in the case of genuine knowledge. Once you have got a moral intuition, it is impossible to doubt what it is that you have; and anything in terms of which you tried to prove its truth would be necessarily less certain than the intuition itself. Of course it is sometimes possible to suffer momentary doubts in matters of behaviour; but these, Prichard says, can be easily set at rest by merely thinking of the matter more carefully.

Suppose we come genuinely to doubt whether we ought to pay our debts, owing to a genuine doubt whether our previous conviction that we ought to do so is true, a doubt which can, in fact, only arise if we fail to remember the real nature of what we now call our past conviction. The only remedy lies in actually getting into a situation which occasions the obligation, or if our imagination be strong enough in imagining ourselves in that situation, and then letting our moral capacities of thinking do their work.[1]

Prichard elaborates these views about moral obligation in a long essay of this title, which appears in the book, and which was apparently designed to form part of a complete book on the subject.[2] In it, he goes into more detail about the relation between obligation and the happiness of the agent, on the one

---

[1] *op. cit.* p. 16.　　　　　　　[2] *op. cit.* pp. 87 *sqq.*

hand, and on the other hand the relation between obligatoriness and the production of good. The essay contains discussion of the views of other moral philosophers, including Plato, Butler, Mill, and Kant. My interest in it is solely to call attention to a curious refinement of his own view about obligation which is to be found in it. He says that the main question to be answered is the question 'What is being under an obligation to do some action?' There are, he says, two possible answers to this. (1) We may say that if X is under an obligation, for instance, to educate Y, then the statement, that he *is* under this obligation, is the ascribing of a predicate to the true subject of the proposition, which is the name of an action, viz. educating Y. On this view, then, the true analysis of the proposition 'X ought to educate Y' would be 'educating Y is obligatory-upon-X'. Alternatively (2) we may hold that the predicate is really to be attached not to the name of the action, but to the name of the agent. Thus the analysis would be 'X is obliged-to-educate-Y'. In the earlier essay, I think that Prichard would have accepted the first of these analyses. But now he sees a difficulty. For he thinks that 'being obligatory-upon-X' cannot really be the name of a quality which is possessed by the education of Y. But *'ought to exist'* can be the name of a quality, and so he thinks 'obligatory-upon-X' must be said to mean the same as 'ought to exist'. But, he says, where we say that something ought to be done, we imply that it has not yet been done; thus in this case we imply that the education of Y has not yet been undertaken, and therefore does not exist. But 'we can no more either think or assert of something which we think does not exist that it ought to exist than we can think or assert anything else about it. Of what we think does not exist, we can think and assert nothing at all.' Therefore the first analysis would have to become 'educating Y would be something which ought to exist, if it existed', which is to make the original statement hypothetical instead of categorical. Therefore the first interpretation must be rejected. This seems to be one of Prichard's odder intuitions. But he repeats it at the end of the essay:

If this idea were true, there could be no such thing as an obligation to do some action until the act is already done, whereas from its very nature there can only be an obligation to do an action as long as it is not done. This must be so because though it may at first escape our notice, only something which *is* can be something which ought or ought not to exist.

This difficulty is generated by the insistence that being obligatory would, if it were a property, be a property like yellowness. For Prichard could hold with some plausibility that if you say of some non-existent object that it is yellow you must be understood to mean either that it was yellow when it did exist, or that it would be yellow if it did exist. But perhaps, equally, the difficulty is caused by thinking of actions as objects which have properties, and do or do not *exist*. In any case, Prichard is forced by these considerations to adopt the second analysis of the proposition that X is under an obligation to educate Y, namely that 'being-under-an-obligation' is a quality of X.

It would be possible to find many more examples of Prichard's technique applied to problems of moral philosophy, but one more will be enough. It turns on the very same problem his solution of which we have just noticed. In an essay entitled 'Duty and Ignorance of Fact', which was delivered as a lecture to the British Academy in 1932,[1] Prichard considers the following problem, 'If a man has an obligation, i.e. a duty, to do some action, does the obligation depend on certain characteristics of the situation in which he is, or on certain characteristics of his thought about the situation?' This second solution, that the obligation depends on his thought, Prichard calls the subjective view, and it is upon this that he finally decides. His progress towards this conclusion is typical not merely of his technique, but of the method of intuitionism as a whole. The first thing to be done, he says, is to ascertain which of the two possible views better corresponds with the thought of our ordinary life. He then suggests with considerable plausibility that both the views correspond to at least part of our ordinary thought about moral situations. We often think without question that the *facts* of the situation are 'what render us bound to do the act' . . . for instance to administer a drug which we know would cure a man who is ill. On the other hand we often think we ought, for instance, to slow down as we approach a main road in our car, not because there *is* traffic on the main road, but because we

[1] *op. cit.* pp. 18 *sqq.*

think there is, or at least may be, traffic. It does not turn out not to have been our duty just because there happens to be nothing coming this time. Prichard will not allow that, in such cases as this, what renders us bound to do the act is a probability. Probabilities, he says, are not facts. To speak of a probability is just a short-hand way of speaking about our *thought* about the situation. If this is agreed, it is fairly easy to see that the subjective view will win. And so it does; but at first there seem to be grave objections to it. One objection raised is that on the subjective view what is my duty in a given situation may not be your duty in the same situation, because our thoughts may be different. Another is that, supposing we were omniscient, then on this view, if we are bound to do something (to shout to revive a fainting man is Prichard's rather surprising example), then what renders us bound to shout is not the fact that shouting would revive him, but our knowledge that it would. Thus knowledge is not knowledge *of* the ground of the obligation, but is itself the ground of the obligation. Knowledge of the ground of the obligation would, if it existed, consist of knowledge that we knew that shouting would cure the man. Prichard then sets about to get over these objections to the subjective view. At first he tries reformulating, in general, all statements about obligations. He considers what is meant by 'acting', and he says that 'we have in the end to allow' that we mean by 'acting' 'bringing about the existence of some new state of affairs'. This we may do either directly or indirectly. 'We think that in moving our head we bring about a change of place of our head directly, whereas in giving a friend the family news we bring about his receipt of the news indirectly, i.e. by bringing about directly certain other changes which in turn cause it.' Confining his attention to those cases of actions which are 'bringing about directly', even here he thinks that there is a further distinction which we all of us make:

In no case whatever, where we think of ourselves as having brought about something directly, do we think that our activity was that of bringing about that something. On the contrary we think of the activity as having been of another sort, and mean by saying that we brought about directly what we did, that this activity of another sort had the change in question as a direct effect.

This activity which we *really* think that we performed is the activity of 'setting ourselves' to bring about the change we did bring about. Similarly, if we claim that we *can* do something in the future, what we mean is that we can set ourselves to do that thing; and if now we say we are obliged to do something, what we mean is not that we are obliged to *do* it, but that we are obliged to *set ourselves* to do it. This, Prichard admits, is contrary to the implication of ordinary language; but in this case ordinary language apparently fails to do justice to what we think. If we reformulate the original question about obligation in terms of obligation to set ourselves to bring things about, then Prichard thinks that the objective view, according to which the grounds of the obligation are facts, is rendered less plausible. For since it is acknowledged that setting ourself to do something may not have any effect at all (we may become paralysed quite suddenly), it is less plausible to think that our obligation must rest on the fact that what we are obliged to do will have some particular effect. It can only rest on the fact that we think it will probably have some effect. But the difficulties in the subjective view remain. For an obligation to do an action seems, he says, to be a characteristic of the action, and therefore *cannot* depend on whether we think it likely that the action has the characteristic; it must depend on its actually having it. And it makes no difference to this difficulty whether we are to characterize doing something or setting ourselves to do something as obligatory.

Finally, he resolves the difficulty in the way we have considered already. He decides that it is a mistake after all to consider obligatoriness as a characteristic of actions. Rather we should think of being-under-an-obligation as a characteristic of people. If this is right, and being under an obligation is a characteristic of ourselves, there is nothing to prevent the presence of this characteristic in us being dependent on some thoughts we may have about the situation we are in. 'Indeed,' Prichard says, 'its existence *must* depend on some fact about ourselves.' Thus the fundamental difficulty which seemed to stand in the way of accepting the subjective view has suddenly been dissolved. It remains only, Prichard says, to take some actual case, to consider what we ought to do, and then to ask ourselves whether in fact, in that particular case, the subjective or the objective view was true. Did we, that is, make our decision on the facts of the case, or on what we thought about the facts? Here Prichard engagingly tells us that there is little that need be said,[1] 'For we have only to carry out this procedure to find not that we are *inclined to think*, or even that we are of the opinion that, but that we are *certain*, i.e. *know* that the answer turns not on the nature of the situation but on that of our thought about it.'

So the problem posed at the beginning of the essay is solved. We may be inclined to ask why, if this simple introspective method was to be so successful in the end, it could not be applied at the beginning. But the problem has first to be defined clearly. Next we have to consider what we would ordinarily think about its solution. If difficulties seem, as they did here, to be generated by what we would ordinarily think, we have to think further what we really mean when we use certain of the expressions involved. At this stage in the argument, Prichard is not merely consulting ordinary use, nor what the plain man would say. He is prepared to legislate: we ought to think of being obliged as a characteristic of people, and not of obligatoriness as a characteristic of actions, even if we do not think this at first. The reason is that problems are resolved by the proper way of thinking, or rather they need never arise. In order to bring out the proper way of looking at the matter he suggests that it is better to use the form of words 'I ought to do X' rather than the form 'X is right'. Then, once these confusions have been cleared out of the way, simple inspection of the facts will indeed be sufficient to solve the original problem. We have not exactly progressed. It is rather that the object we started by looking at has been stripped of its obscuring and confusing covers so that now one quick look will be enough to tell us its true nature. But all the same, doubts may remain; and for two reasons. First we may doubt whether the object we were required to look at was really worth it. Do we, or can we, care very much about the solution to Prichard's problems? Secondly, we may doubt whether we are really seeing so clearly in the end. Prichard pushes us through the argument

[1] *op. cit.* p. 38.

with a great deal of energy. But it is doubtful whether we want to admit all the things he says we must admit, or whether we really do think all the things he tells us we think. It is here that the appalling weakness of Prichard's position lies. If a problem is supposed to be solved by the consideration of common sense and what people ordinarily think, then not only has the problem to be one which people would be ordinarily prepared to think about, but what they would ordinarily say and think must be truly stated. It is not in fact so easy as Prichard seems to think, to say *what* our moral vocabulary means or *what* our moral concepts are. It is all very well to ride roughshod over ordinary language; this may often be necessary and desirable for philosophers. But it is in the highest degree undesirable to do this in the name of ordinary language itself.

With Prichard, then, the intuitive clarity of his conclusions turns out to be a fake clarity; and there is a good deal of bluster in the assurance with which he finally states the conclusions themselves.

If we turn now to Ross, the tone is very different. I shall discuss, very briefly, Ross's book *The Foundations of Ethics*. This was published in 1939, and is based on the Gifford Lectures, delivered in 1935. Ross says of his book that it is to be a critical study 'of the moral consciousness and of the main moral theories'. In fact the ground it covers is not quite so wide as this description might make us hope. But the topics which he selected to discuss were those which seemed central to the whole of this group of intuitionist philosophers. The task of moral philosophers, Ross held, is to resolve the difficulties into which plain men might fall if they considered, not this or that particular moral problem, but the status of those moral principles which they would use to settle *any* moral problem. People may become confused by the fact that their principles, none of which perhaps they want to give up, may conflict in some cases; they may find, for instance, that they cannot tell the truth without endangering someone's life, or they cannot keep a promise without telling a lie. Another source of confusion may be that they see that principles change at different times, and are different in different societies. It is to the solution of such general difficulties as these that moral philosophers should address themselves.

As regards the first problem, that of the conflict of principles, Ross holds that principles cannot survive if they are taken to be absolute.

The only way to save the authority of such rules is to recognize them not as rules guaranteeing the rightness of any act that falls under them, but as rules guaranteeing that any act which falls under them tends so far as that aspect of its nature goes, to be right, and can be rendered wrong only if in virtue of another aspect of its nature it comes under another rule by reason of which it tends more decidedly to be wrong.

Kant, Ross says, overshot the mark in saying that principles could be absolute. But the trouble is that it would be hard not to overshoot the mark which Ross has set before us. If you shoot at all you are sure to go too far. Intuitionism has here lost all its dash; we are to be so cautious in stating moral principles that they will scarcely serve us as guides at all. The second puzzle, that of the relativity of moral principles, is to be dealt with by grading principles in order of self-evidence. There are some which appear, according to Ross, to be completely self-evident, and can never be given up. Such, for instance, is the principle that we should produce as much good as we can. Ross does not, I think, mean to suggest that even this principle can *never* conflict with any other, for later he says that it might conflict with the principle of keeping promises. It is only that no consideration of the morals of another age or society would ever make us doubt whether this is a moral principle at all. No doubt this is correct; at least it is very natural to regard it as true by definition that it is a moral duty to produce as much good as possible. This at any rate was Moore's view (though admittedly not Ross's). But just because of the tautological nature of this rule, it is not very likely that we shall find any disputes centring upon it. The top grade of principles, therefore, even if there are more of them than this one, is not likely to be very helpful. The second grade is made up of those principles which can be derived from the first by reference to general truths about human nature; the third grade is of principles derived from the first by reference to the particular circumstances which obtain in any given period or place; the fourth and last grade is of principles wrongly derived from the first by reference to false opinions about human nature.

In order to help non-philosophers in these and perhaps other ways, Ross says that it is further necessary for philosophers to consider moral words, and moral characteristics. Moral words should be considered in their actual use; but this study, Ross suggests, is more properly lexicography than philosophy. It is, as we should by now expect, to the study of moral characteristics that the philosopher is really supposed to devote himself. If you take any moral characteristic, there seem to be three questions which, Ross says, we should answer with regard to it. The first question is whether or not it exists at all; the second is what is its nature; and the third is what objects are possessed of it. Ross himself attempts to answer these questions first about the characteristic 'rightness' and then about 'goodness'. To take 'rightness' first: we are told that it is self-evident that rightness exists since it is self-evident that there are many situations in which there would be one right thing to do. We see in a moral situation a number of prima facie duties, that is, things which at first glance seem right, because they fall under some moral principle. And because these prima facie duties exist, 'we see that there must be some action which would have a higher degree of resultant suitability than any of the other actions that could be done in the circumstances, though we may have no certainty as to which action would have this characteristic'. Regarding a moral situation that is, is enough to assure us that there is *something* which is right, though not to assure us *what* is right. As a matter of fact it is not obvious *either* that we always suppose that there is something which it would be right to do, *or* that we therefore think of rightness as a characteristic of anything. Ross assumes that we do both these things, and so the next step is to reflect on the nature of this characteristic. Ross examines a number of attempts to define 'right', doing for it rather what Moore does for 'good', and concludes that rightness is indefinable; and even if it can be put into some more general category such as 'suitability', its differentia cannot be stated, 'just as while red is a species of colour, what distinguishes it from other colours can be indicated only by saying that it is the colour that is red'. As to what things have this indefinable characteristic, Ross allows that a number of things may be said to possess it, but that *properly* only actions, acts of self-exertion, are right. Like Prichard, Ross is inclined to be cautious about saying that a whole overt action can be right, since he, like Prichard, thinks that the whole complete action contains some elements for which we are not responsible, or rather that there are some aspects of an action which it is not in our power to bring about. Once again, the spectre of paralysis is made to haunt us. It cannot be that moving my arm is what is right, since suddenly I may not be able to do so much, and still I may have done right. What is right is exerting myself or setting myself to move my arm. This is the general nature of the things which may qualify to have the characteristic of rightness. But Ross goes on to ask *how* they qualify. This is surprising, since we have already been told that rightness is indefinable. And, as one would expect, the answer to the question is negative. It is not only, and not always, the fact that they lead to the production of good that makes right actions right; what it is that makes them right has to be grasped intuitively, from a general consideration of the circumstances. Once again we are offered the analogy with mathematics: 'We see the predicate, though not included in the definition of the subject, to belong necessarily to anything which satisfies that definition.' But Ross suggests that, if anything, we can be *more* certain of the truths of ethics than of the truths of mathematics, since, whereas in mathematics we have to make do with diagrams which are less than perfect representations of true circles or squares, in ethics we can find actual examples of cruelty, generosity, promise-keeping, and the other subjects of ethical propositions.

From 'right' Ross moves on to 'good'. 'Good', he says, is used in two main senses, 'good as means' and 'good as an end' or 'good in itself'. Ruling out the first sense as of no interest to ethics, Ross sub-divides the second sense into 'good' meaning 'worthy of interest' and 'good' meaning 'worthy of admiration'. In both these senses 'goodness' is the name of a quality; but in the sense of 'worthy of interest' it is a quality which can be recognized only by reference to rightness, for a thing is good in this sense if and only if it is such that interest in it would, if it existed, be 'right or morally suitable'. The primary quality of goodness, however, that is, the quality of being *worthy of admiration*, is recognizable only by a separate intuition. Finally Ross tries to throw light on the question what things have this characteristic of goodness. The answer is that various interests, motives, and desires are the things which possess the characteristic. Kant was wrong to say that only the disinterested desire to do one's duty was good; Ross suggests instead that it is the best of all motives or desires, but may be made better still by the addition of some other good motive, such as the desire to give pleasure to others, or the desire to improve our own characters.

In the whole book, the only arguments we find are those directed to the refutation of the views of other philosophers; for Ross, like Prichard and Moore, could not consistently argue for views which were supposed either to be self-evidently true, or at least certain, if one thought about the matter clearly. But Ross does not speak with the passion of Moore nor with the frenetic emphasis of Prichard. His is a cool voice simply making statements, dividing, sub-dividing, and categorizing. He says that we know the truths of ethics as we know the truths of mathematics, even perhaps better; but what we know suddenly seems to be rather boring: we know that we should do good; we know that we should keep promises, at least as long as nothing very important stands in the way of keeping them; we know that we should take an interest in the pleasures of others, but not in our own pleasures; we know that we should try to improve ourselves. Rightness and goodness are the two moral properties with which Ross is concerned. Both of these have to be intuitively grasped when they are present in a thing. But we can of course, with long experience, come to make inductive generalizations about moral matters. For instance, if we have frequently observed cases of lying and noticed that among their other qualities they have the quality of moral wrongness, then we can generalize and say 'lying is wrong'. This, then, becomes a moral rule, if we convert it to the legitimate form 'we ought not to lie', and this moral rule binds us, though not absolutely. We have a prima facie duty to obey it. If we wish not to, the onus is on us to show why not. For of course moral generalizations, like any generalization, are fallible and may not apply exactly in every case. So we may have to apply our intuitive faculty again to the individual case before us, to see whether perhaps, in this case, we can detect moral rightness instead of moral wrongness in the lie. Ross is not even *certain* that rightness is indefinable. He thinks that it is, but he is at least prepared for us, if we choose, to use a synonym, namely 'moral fittingness, or moral suitability'. These permitted synonyms seem to me to be revealing. The intuitive powers which are ascribed to us by Ross are very small powers; and they will work only in well-worn fields. The concept of the fitting or the suitable is a concept properly applied in cases where we know our way around pretty well. They suggest a set of conventions, any breach of which will be immediately detected by us. They suggest, just as Bradley suggested before, that we each of us have our place and our position, to which some behaviour is proper, some is not. But suppose all these conventions and systems break up? Shall we still know what is fitting? I do not see how we could be expected to. I do not know what is fitting behaviour in a prison camp or in an occupied country, even though I may know what is fitting in my role of housewife or college tutor. It is not accidental that in both Prichard and Ross we notice the examples grow more and more trivial and absurd. It is difficult to imagine feeling very greatly exercised about whether to shout to revive a fainting man, whether to slow down as we approach the main road in our car, or whether to return the book that we have borrowed. It is no comfort in cases like these to be told that we need only set ourselves to do them, and that we shall not be blamed if we do not thereafter succeed. We do not want comfort in these cases. Perhaps if Bradley had said that it was enough to set ourselves to possess the whole universe, we should have been grateful that we did not have to succeed. But when it comes to returning what we have borrowed, if not only is this a fair example of our duties, but if we need not actually succeed in doing even so much, then we begin to feel that the intuitionists' moral philosophy is a cheat. It does not really deal with the subject we had been led to expect. There may always be a step to be taken between saying that an action has any characteristic at all and saying that we should do it; and we may need intuition to help us to take the step. But if the actions are so obvious or so farcical, the intuition cannot be much of a thing either. If moral philosophy had always been based on a mistake, perhaps the best course would have been to stop doing it. It is certainly difficult to see that much more of it could profitably have been undertaken in this particular way.

4

The Emotive Theory

IN 1936, three years before the publication of *The Foundations of Ethics*, *Language, Truth and Logic* was published. No book has more clearly called for metaphorical description. It was obviously a bombshell. Ayer made no particular claims to originality. In the preface to the first edition he said: 'The views which are put forward in this treatise derive from the doctrines of Bertrand Russell and Wittgenstein, which are themselves the logical outcome of the empiricism of Berkeley and David Hume.' And it is true that the book is firmly in the empiricist tradition. But he goes on himself to say that the philosophers with whom he was in closest agreement were the logical positivists; and the tremendous impact of the book was largely due to its being the first, and most brilliant, exposition of their views to be published in England.

The book contains one chapter on ethics, which is entitled 'Critique of Ethics and Theology'.[1] It is superbly short, less than twenty pages. Ayer's general contention is, briefly, that any statement which has meaning must fall into one of two categories. Either it must be analytic, that is necessarily true but not concerned with empirical matters of fact; or it must be empirical. If it is empirical, it can never be more than probable; it is, in fact, a hypothesis. Both the meaning and the probability of the hypothesis are established by empirical verification. That is to say, if a statement is to qualify for the second category, it must be capable of verification by sense-experience. According to this theory, then, no statement can be said to have any mean-

[1] *Language, Truth and Logic*, chapter 6.

ing which is not either analytic, or verifiable by observation of the world. The propositions of logic and mathematics, and all definitions of symbols, fall into the first category; the propositions of science and of ordinary life, in so far as these simply state matters of fact, fall into the second category. There are no other categories. It can be seen at once that this creates a problem for ethics. Ethical propositions, such as that theft is wrong, or that generosity is to be encouraged, do not come under either of the possible headings. No one would wish to say that such statements were analytic; they do not, in Ayer's words, 'simply record our determination to use symbols in a certain fashion'. But it would be equally implausible to suggest that they were capable of verification by ordinary sense-experience. Even the most enthusiastic intuitionist would never maintain that one literally saw or heard the goodness of an action or motive. In Chapter 6 of *Language, Truth and Logic* Ayer sets out to deal with this problem. 'It is our business,' he says, 'to give an account of "judgements of value" which is both satisfactory in itself and consistent with our general empiricist principles.'

Ayer first considers the suggestion that, while ethical propositions cannot be directly verified by appeal to sense-experience, yet they can be translated without loss into propositions which can be so verified. If this suggestion were accepted, value judgements would be saved, since they could fit ultimately, though not immediately, into the second class of meaningful statements. Ayer considers two versions of this view, which he calls, respectively, subjectivism and utilitarianism. Subjectivists hold that to say a thing is right is to say that it is generally approved of, or alternatively that it is approved of by the speaker. Ayer rejects this view, on the grounds that it cannot *mean the same* to say the one as to say the other, since it is possible without contradiction to say of something that it is both generally approved of and wrong. And even if the extreme subjectivist view is taken, still it is not actually contradictory to say 'I approve of this and it is wrong.' Ayer therefore rejects the contention that ethical predicates such as 'right' or 'good' can be translated into the empirical predicates 'approved of by everybody' or 'approved of by me'. On exactly the same grounds he rejects utilitarianism. Since it is not actually a contradiction to say that it is sometimes wrong to perform the action which would cause the greatest happiness, 'right action' and 'action causing the greatest happiness' cannot mean the same. For it *would* be contradictory to say 'It is sometimes wrong to perform the right action.' It is therefore shown, Ayer thinks, that no translation of ethical terms into empirical terms is possible.

It looks at first as though the only alternative to the naturalism thus rejected is what Ayer calls 'absolutism': 'the view that statements of value are not controlled by observation as ordinary empirical propositions are, but only by a mysterious "intellectual intuition"'. But to accept this would obviously be incompatible with the general theory that the only significant non-analytic propositions are those which are empirically verifiable. Therefore Ayer rejects absolutism too and adopts a third theory. Ethical concepts are agreed to be unanalysable but this is because they are not real concepts at all. They are 'pseudo-concepts'. The predicates used in value judgements are not proper predicates; they do not stand for qualities of things which can be picked out by the senses.

The presence [Ayer says] of an ethical symbol in a proposition adds nothing to its factual content. . . . If I say to someone 'you acted wrongly in stealing that money', I am not stating anything more than if I had simply said 'you stole that money'. In adding that this action is wrong I am simply evincing my moral disapproval of it.

And so, if nothing is stated in any given proposition except that something is wrong it follows that nothing is stated in it at all. If for instance I say not 'you were wrong to steal the money' where at least 'you stole the money' purports to be true, but 'stealing money is wrong', then what I have said 'expresses no proposition which can be either true or false'. I have done *nothing* but evince my moral disapproval, and the question of truth or falsehood does not arise. It follows from this, in accordance with the general verification theory, that a pure value judgement does not qualify as a meaningful statement at all. It plainly is not analytic; nor does it come into the second class of meaningful statements, for the good reason that it is not a statement, and therefore cannot, naturally, be verified. 'If a sentence makes no statement at all, there is obviously no sense in asking whether what it says is true or false.' It follows further, on Ayer's view, that it is impossible for two people to contradict each other on points of morals (or indeed of aesthetics either, for all value judgements are analysed in the same way). Nor am I contradicting myself if I say first that something is right and then that it is wrong. All I am doing by using the words 'right' and 'wrong' is expressing my ethical feelings. I am not stating that I have certain feelings, for if I were, I could contradict myself in saying that I had them and that I did not have them at the same time. But expressions of feeling are not assertions, and though they may suggest a contradiction (as laughing and crying together might be thought to), they cannot actually contradict each other. It is not possible, therefore, to argue about questions of value; the most we can do is continue to express ourselves, and give vent to our emotions.

This, then, is the bald statement of Ayer's view, which he offers as an alternative to both absolutism and naturalism. In passing, Ayer adds a further refinement, which turns out, in the later development of the theory, to be very important. 'It is worth mentioning,' he says, 'that ethical terms do not serve only to express feeling. They are calculated also to arouse feeling, and so to stimulate action. Indeed some of them are used in such a way as to give the sentences in which they occur the effect of commands.' He goes on to distinguish ethical terms one from another by the forcefulness of the command contained in the meaning of each. Thus 'duty' contains an emphatic command, 'ought' a less emphatic one, and 'good' contains scarcely any element of command at all.

It is obvious that what we have in *Language, Truth and Logic* is a sketch of an ethical theory, rather than a complete theory. In the years that followed there was a considerable number of articles by various philosophers, all of them filling in the gaps, and elaborating the details of this kind of theory. But, though I shall say something about some of these in the second half of this chapter, I want to stop for a moment to consider the theory as it was presented by Ayer. It is not unfair to him, I think, to regard this chapter as a statement of view rather than as an argument, and a view which could properly be said to be that of a school of philosophy. It is part of the measure of the importance of his book that no sooner was it published than it seemed that emotivists in ethics were everywhere. They had not been converted by the book; it was their creed already. For instance thirteen years before *Language, Truth and Logic* came out, Ogden and Richards published their famous book, *The Meaning of Meaning*. They first introduced the word 'emotive' and used it in just the way that Ayer did. And their ethical theory, being derived from the same sources, and the outcome of the very same influences, is, even verbally, very close to his. One quotation will be enough to show this:

'Good' is alleged to stand for a unique, unanalysable concept . . . [which] is the subject matter of ethics. When so used the word stands for nothing whatever, and has no symbolic function. Thus when we use it in the sentence 'This is good' we merely refer to *this* and the addition of 'is good' makes no difference whatever to our reference. When, on the other hand, we say 'This is red', the addition of 'is red' to '*this*' does symbolize an extension of our reference, namely to some other red thing. But 'is good' has no comparable *symbolic* function: it serves only as an emotive sign expressing our attitude to *this* and perhaps evoking similar attitudes in other persons, or inciting them to actions of one kind or another.[1]

The extreme simplicity of Ayer's remarks about ethics (which he himself called attention to in the preface to the 1947 edition of the book), as well as their brevity, made them peculiarly suitable as dogma, and this is what emotivism, in one form or another, became.

Two preliminary points should be made. First, there is no purpose in discussing the almost hysterical fury with which the doctrines of *Language, Truth and Logic* were greeted in some quarters. On the whole, the rage was in inverse proportion to the intelligence of the attack. Logical positivists were accused not so much of being mistaken as of being wicked. They were held actually responsible for the greatest evils of the twentieth century. It is easy to see why. The verification principle entailed the total dismissal of metaphysics; and with metaphysics had to go the propositions of religion. Even ethical and aesthetic

[1] *The Meaning of Meaning*, p. 125.

propositions were, as we have seen, said to be literally meaningless. It is not surprising that people felt called upon to defend their most deeply held convictions. Moreover, the whole point of the book was polemical. No doubt Ayer aimed to upset people, and he admirably succeeded. But by now we can distinguish this temporary and therapeutic aim from the question of the actual truth or falsity of the doctrines. We can try to interpret the language of 'pseudo-concepts' and 'nonsense' soberly, and without emotion. No doubt the verification principle, as a theory of meaning, was grotesquely narrow and limited in its applicability. But our concern here is not with this general question but with the emotive theory of ethics itself. And this leads to my second preliminary point. In the chapter on 'Ethics', Ayer, perhaps unwisely, presents his case for emotivism as though it rested primarily on a desire to find an ethical theory which would not conflict with the general verification doctrine. He wrote almost as if any theory would do, so long as it was consistent with the rest of the book. In particular, he appears to reject what he calls absolutism on the grounds that to accept it 'would undermine the whole of our main argument'. Criticisms of the emotive theory have therefore sometimes taken the form simply of criticisms of the verification principle, in the mistaken belief that if this were refuted, there would be no further reason for even considering an emotive theory. Thus Ross in *The Foundations of Ethics* seems to regard the emotive theory as an attempt to 'discredit ethics', which would never have been undertaken if it had not been for the demands of logical positivism as a whole. Both parts of this criticism are misguided, though both are understandable, considering the general iconoclastic tone of *Language, Truth and Logic*. In the introduction to the second edition, Ayer notices that Ross and others have treated the ethical theory as though it were a mere corollary of the verification principle, and he denies that this is so. He says that even if the verification principle is rejected there are still good reasons for accepting an emotive theory of ethics. But naturally he cannot there go into the question of what these good reasons are. But at any rate it is clear that we are justified in considering the theory by itself and on its own merits. It is not *mere* iconoclasm, nor is it a theory just put together for the purposes of a particular argument. It is far more plausible and more serious than either of these descriptions would suggest. Of course there is an important connexion between the emotive theory, and Ayer's general epistemological views. It is only the particular presentation of the connexion which might be called into question.

The most obvious feature of the theory is its firm rejection of naturalism. Moore's formula for the rejection of naturalistic and other definitions of 'good' was as follows: of any proposed definition—let us call the defining phrase D—you could always intelligibly ask 'Is D good?' And this showed that you were not really treating D as equivalent to 'good'. Ayer's formula is that for any proposed definition D, you could always deny without contradiction that it was good, and therefore you could not be using D as equivalent to good. Ayer argues, that is, that it makes sense to deny of any empirical characteristic whatever that it is good; Moore argues that it makes sense in every case to *raise the question* of denying it. Thus Ayer, like Moore, bases his rejection of naturalism on logical grounds. It would be perfectly open to him to use the phrase 'naturalistic fallacy'; and indeed the phrase has come to be used far more often than not in the context of some sort of emotive theory, in which the alternative to accepting a naturalistic definition of ethical terms is to say that ethical terms are emotive, or at any rate non-descriptive. This leaves the question whether they can be defined at all somewhat unclear. Ayer, whose version of the theory we are still considering, is careful to distinguish normative, or properly ethical, uses of ethical terms from descriptive uses. I may say that something is good and mean *nothing more* than that it is enjoined by a certain code; at least this is what he claims. In this case I am using 'good' descriptively, and in this use it *can* be defined. But if I use 'good' properly, then in using it I am merely expressing my feelings. In this use 'good' cannot be defined, because it does not stand for any concept which could be analysed. Therefore in the sense in which definition is equivalent to analysis, 'good' is indefinable, necessarily. But that is not to say that I could not be taught when it was proper to use the word. There are conventions governing the use of ejaculations, and these can be explained. Saying 'That's bad' when I felt pleased by something would be inappropriate and misleading in exactly the same way as saying 'hooray' when I stubbed my toe would be. 'Hooray' or 'damn' cannot be defined, because they do not stand for characteristics of things. When we utter them we are not stating facts about things but expressing our feelings. The *names* of feelings can of course be defined, and in using *them* I am making factual statements. Thus, if I say 'I am very much put out,' what I say may be true or false. Another way of saying that it may, is to say that 'very much put out' stands for a concept, and concepts can be analysed. But 'damn' does not *stand for* anything. The position of ethical terms is the same.

It can perhaps be seen now that the difference between Ayer and Moore is far and away greater and more important than is the agreement between them. In spite of the close similarity in the actual form of their rejection of naturalism, even their purposes in rejecting it are wholly different. Moore's main concern is to state what are the things which are good in themselves. His interest in the *language* of ethics is simply preliminary to this. He needs to expose the mistakes of others in their treatment of the concept of 'goodness', in order to expound the truth; and this truth is not primarily a truth about words at all, but a genuinely ethical truth. This fact cannot be too strongly emphasized. Those philosophers who conceive the business of ethics to be the analysis of the language of morals are not following Moore, though they may claim to do so; but they are, on the other hand, in the true logical positivist tradition. Ayer is perfectly explicit about the task of moral philosophy. He divides ethical propositions into four main classes. There are propositions which express definitions of ethical terms, there are propositions which describe moral experience, there are exhortations to virtue, and finally there are actual ethical judgements, that such and such a thing is good or is bad. 'In fact,' he says, 'it is easy to see that only the first of our four classes, namely that which comprises the propositions relating to the definitions of ethical terms, can be said to constitute ethical philosophy.' Descriptions of moral experience are matters for psychology or anthropology; and the two remaining classes turn out really to be one. For exhortations to virtue would doubtless be agreed not only to urge other people to action, but also to express the speaker's feelings about the action; and we have already seen that ethical judgements proper, when analysed, emerge as combined expression of feeling and command or exhortation. Now it was absolutely to be expected that Ayer should regard the function of moral philosophers in this light. It is demanded by his theory of the function of philosophy in general. In the preface to the first edition of *Language, Truth and Logic*, having explained that any proposition which fails to pass the test of empirical verifiability is literally senseless, Ayer says 'it will be found that much of what ordinarily passes for philosophy is metaphysics (i.e. senseless) according to this criterion and, in particular, that it cannot be significantly asserted that there is a non-empirical world of values . . .' and he adds that the philosopher's function is 'to clarify the propositions of science by exhibiting their logical relationships and by defining the symbols which occur in them'. The moral philosopher, then, has first to show that the propositions of morals are not scientific, that is, that they do not state empirical facts, and has then to analyse the terms which they do contain. When this has been done, his task is over. What is perhaps surprising, to look a little ahead, is that this task of analysis of the words of ethics should have continued for so long to dominate English and American moral philosophy. Admittedly great subtleties of analysis turned out to be possible, which were not apparent in the first sketch. But the dogma of the limits of the task—the insistence that one could first mark off ethical propositions from all others and then show how they work, and that this was moral philosophy—these assumptions seem to have outlived the general beliefs about the nature of philosophy out of which they originally arose.

As to the actual analysis which Ayer proposed, the emotive theory itself, this has great plausibility and appeal for any empiricist. Ayer was perfectly right to insist on his empiricist ancestry. For instance Berkeley, in the introduction to the *Principles of Human Knowledge*, distinguished four different 'ends of language' and suggested that there were more. Besides the communicating of ideas, 'There are other ends, as the raising of some passion, the exciting to or deterring from some action, the putting the mind in some particular disposition.' And Berkeley mentions the word 'good' and the word 'danger' as examples of words which may be so used. The word 'good' may raise a passion without there being any particular characteristic which is referred to by its use. More important is the tradition of Hume. Hume insisted that moral judgements were neither necessary and *a priori*, nor were they descriptions of any actual feature of the world. All that there really is in the world is a series of sense impressions, and whereas we have actual sense impressions of the physical characteristics of things, their moral value is not among these characteristics. When, therefore, we use ethical or aesthetic terms we are not directly referring to things in the world, but to our own attitude towards these things. We have seen that Ayer rejected what he called the subjectivist view that to say something is good is the same as to say that it is approved of, and I suppose that this is the doctrine he would ascribe to Hume. In fact I think Hume did not mean precisely this, but for our present purposes the details of his doctrine are irrelevant. What is clear is that Ayer shares Hume's basic conviction that value is not part of the world. This is the fundamental feature of those empirical theories of morals which have had the most powerful influence in the twentieth century and whose most dramatic statement is to be found at the end of Wittgenstein's *Tractatus*:

The sense of the world must lie outside the world. In the world everything is as it is and happens as it does happen. In it there is no value—and if there were it would be of no value. If there is any value which is of value, it must lie outside all happening and being so. For all happening and being so is accidental.

The logical positivists were professionally interested only in scientific, fact-stating discourse. They thought that such discourse could be marked off once and for all from other uses of language, and they further thought that these other uses, in so far as they often masqueraded as fact-stating when they were not, were actually vicious. This explains the hostility, in *Language, Truth and Logic*, implicit in such expressions as 'pseudo-concepts' and so on. This explains why Wittgenstein in the

Tractatus said that there could be no propositions of ethics. It explains, finally, why having roughly characterized ethical language as emotive, in very much the same way as Berkeley had, Ayer displays very little further interest in it. His purpose was negative; he wanted to clear the field for significant discourse, and what was thrown out, provided it was shown to be truly non-scientific, was not worth examining very closely. Although as we shall see in a moment, the first crudity of the emotive theory was rubbed off very soon, what was not questioned was the distinction between descriptive and evaluative language. The belief that somewhere behind all discourse there lay a pure array of facts, with pure fact-stating statements belonging to it with which evaluative statements could be contrasted—this belief seems to have had a far longer life in the field of ethics than anywhere else.

I want now to turn to the later developments of the emotive theory. Inevitably a lot of interesting and subtle work will be left out altogether here. All that I can hope to do is to show how the theory developed as it came into contact with various other philosophical tendencies, and as philosophers came to be interested in it for its own sake. The most important name in the history of this development is that of the American philosopher C. L. Stevenson. In 1937 he published in *Mind* an article entitled 'The Emotive Meaning of Ethical Terms', which was of the greatest importance.[1] I shall consider the arguments contained in this article in some detail. Stevenson says that ethical questions take the form 'Is so and so good?' The aim of his article is to make such ethical questions clear. He sets out a list of requirements which, he says, it has been generally and rightly assumed need to be fulfilled by any satisfactory definition of the word 'good'. These are, first, that on any analysis one must be able to disagree about whether something is good or not; secondly, that 'goodness' must have a certain magnetism. That is, to be told that something is good must at least have a tendency to make one act in its favour. Thirdly, the presence or absence of goodness in a thing must not be verifiable by the use of any scientific method. Stevenson claims that there is some one sense of 'good' which satisfies all

[1] *Mind*, Volume XLVI, pp. 14 *sqq.*

these requirements, and this is the sense analysed by the help of the word 'emotive'. He describes this theory as a kind of interest theory; that is, it is related to the theories of Hobbes and Hume. But whereas traditional interest theories have assumed that ethical statements are descriptions of existing states of interest (for instance that the speaker approves or that people in general approve of whatever is under discussion), the emotive theory recognizes that 'the major use of ethical judgements is to create an interest'. It is the emphasis upon description, he says, which renders all the traditional theories irrelevant as analyses of the word 'good'. All this is familiar. There is nothing here, except the air of caution and moderation, which is not in *Language, Truth and Logic*. But Stevenson goes on to raise two further questions of considerable importance. The first is the question how an ethical sentence acquires its power, and the second is, what this influence has to do with the meaning of the sentence. It is to this second question that he goes on to address himself.

Stevenson starts by distinguishing the descriptive from the dynamic use of words. It is important that he is so far saying nothing about the meaning of words, but only about the various uses to which they may be put. Thus, if I know that my companion has a horror of moths, I may say 'moth' not to describe what I see, nor even to inform him that there is a moth in the railway carriage, but specifically in order to get him to leave. Stevenson does not deny that in such a case the word 'moth' does also describe or inform; in fact its dynamic purpose would fail if its ordinary meaning were not understood. His point is simply that we may use the very same words either to inform, or to arouse sympathy, or to drop hints, and so on. He defines the meaning of a word as the psychological causes and effects with which its utterance *tends* to be associated. The meaning, he says, is a causal or dispositional property of the word. There is then, on this interpretation of meaning, a kind of meaning particularly associated with dynamic uses. This is to be called emotive meaning. (The term, as we have seen, was originally used by Ogden and Richards in *The Meaning of Meaning*, but it soon passed into current philosophical language.) 'The emotive meaning of a word is the tendency of a word, arising through the history of its usage, to produce (result from) affective responses in people', and again,

Certain words, because of their emotive meaning, are suited to a certain kind of dynamic use—so well suited, in fact, that the hearer is likely to be misled if we use them in any other way. The more pronounced a word's emotive meaning is, the less likely people are to use it purely descriptively.

The relation between dynamic use and emotive meaning is contingent, not necessary. But it is a very important relation. If in defining a word with emotive meaning, such as the word 'good', the emotive element of the meaning is left out, people are deceived into thinking that the word is most often used descriptively, while in fact it is most often used dynamically. Stevenson goes on to apply this general principle to the particular question of defining 'good'. He concludes that it is impossible to define it exactly; for in any proposed analysis of its meaning the emotive element, though it may not be left out, will be distorted. Thus he suggests that the meaning of 'This is good' is more or less the same as the meaning of 'I like this. Like it as well.' But in the latter phrase the element of command is explicit, whereas in 'This is good' it is implicit. The emotive force of 'This is good' is therefore subtle while in the supposed analysis it is crude. Nevertheless, Stevenson is not worried by the ultimate failure to find an exact equivalent for 'good'.

It is possible [he says] to say that 'this is good' is *about* the favourable interest of the speaker and the hearer . . . and that it has a pleasing emotive meaning which fits the words for use in suggestion. This is a rough description of meaning not a definition. But it serves the same clarifying function that a definition ordinarily does; and that, after all, is enough.

All the requirements with which he started are satisfied by this account of the meaning of 'good'. It is possible for people to disagree about whether something is good, since it is clear that people can have divergent interests. Obviously the requirement that 'good' should have magnetic force is satisfied, for this is precisely what the emotive part of its meaning is. The last requirement was that the presence or absence of goodness in a thing should not be able to be settled by purely scientific methods, and this too is plainly satisfied. If I am commanding you to like something by telling you that it is good, the question how I get to know that it is good need not arise. On the other hand empirical investigations are not wholly ruled out by this analysis since I may offer reasons for issuing the command, and what I give as reasons may be checked by empirical means. Thus if I say 'This book is good, because it will make you laugh,' while you cannot verify the command aspect of my statement, you can find out whether or not the book does make you laugh. Finally Stevenson, like Ayer, insists that the function of moral philosophy is precisely to do what he has embarked on in this article, to analyse the meaning of ethical terms.

If 'X is good' is essentially a vehicle for suggestion, it is scarcely a statement which philosophers, any more than many other men, are called upon to make. To the extent that ethics predicates the ethical terms of anything, rather than explains their meaning, it ceases to be a reflective study.

The alternatives envisaged for moral philosophy are either to tell people what things are good, which it has no right to do, or to tell people what 'good' means, which Stevenson has done.

In the next year, Stevenson published two more articles in *Mind*,[1] both of which were intended to show the emotive theory in action, that is in its application to some of the traditional problems of moral philosophy. The articles were entitled 'Ethical Judgments and Avoidability', and 'Persuasive Definitions'. Both were of the greatest importance, in that they filled in yet more details of the theory, and laid down very clearly the path which moral philosophy was supposed to take, if it was to continue in the empiricist tradition.

In 'Ethical Judgments and Avoidability', Stevenson examined the normal assumption that it is only of avoidable actions that it is proper to use ethical predicates such as 'good' or 'bad'. He argues that the true reason for this is that ethical predicates, being intended primarily to influence conduct, would be ineffective, if they were applied in cases where the agent could not avoid acting in the way he did.

But he is careful to allow that, though the normal use of

[1] *Mind*, Volume XLVII, pp. 45 *sqq.* and 331 *sqq.*

words like 'good' and 'bad' is to encourage or deter people with
regard to conduct such as that which is being judged, there are
also other subordinate uses for value judgements. Someone
may, for instance, evaluate somebody else's conduct in a certain
way so that other people will think better of *him* irrespective of
what they think of the agent. This is no doubt true. Doubtless
ethical words, like any other words, can be put to a great
number of different uses. But I suspect that Stevenson has here
partially lost sight of the distinction between the meaning of
words and their use for a certain purpose; for I do not think he
would want to suggest that, for instance, this snobbish use of
ethical words was part of their permanent meaning.

This is a small point, I daresay. More serious is Stevenson's
failure to make convincing the central thesis of the article, that
it is because ethical words function in a certain way that we
cannot apply them to certain things, for instance causally determined or unavoidable behaviour. It is natural to object to this
view that it puts the cart before the horse; and if anyone suggested that there is some deeper connexion between the moral
character of an act and the fact that it is the free choice of the
agent, I do not think that Stevenson would have any argument
to bring against him. At least none is even hinted at here. If it
were true that ethical words were wholly emotive in their
meaning, that they had no descriptive function at all, then it
would perhaps seem likely that this would effectively prevent
their being intelligibly used of actions which could not have
been avoided. But even if this were so, part of the emotive
meaning would presumably be an expression of the speaker's
feelings; and this part might still be called for by anything
whatever, avoidable or not. I may, after all, express, for instance,
disgust at things, such as cockroaches, which I do not regard
as able to be otherwise. Why should I not do the same for human
actions? But in any case, Stevenson is as a rule very careful to
point out that only part of the meaning of any ethical term is
emotive, and if this is so, he has not shown why they may not be
applied to non-avoidable actions and be at least partially
intelligible.

This case does, incidentally, bring out a difference of emphasis, which I think becomes more and more marked, between

the first, crude formulation of the emotive theory, as stated by Ayer, and its refined form in Stevenson's articles. In Ayer's version of the theory, as we have seen, the *main* function of ethical words was said to be to evince or express feelings, and Ayer noticed only more or less in passing that they might also function to arouse similar feelings in others. In this second article of Stevenson's it is particularly clear that, in his view, the main function of ethical language is to influence other people. And though in the first article he had tentatively suggested as an analysis of 'good' 'I like this, do so as well,' the first part of this analysis tends increasingly to be left out of account. This is not really surprising. In the first place the word 'emotive' itself naturally means 'producing' rather than 'expressing' feelings. Secondly, ethical terms, whatever Ayer may have said about them, are so unlike mere expressions of feelings, that this part of the theory, which was more difficult to justify, tended to get left out in its later developments.

Stevenson's third article, entitled 'Persuasive Definitions', which also appeared in *Mind* during 1938, was even more important than its predecessor as an amplification of the emotive theory. Stevenson starts by defining a persuasive definition as one which gives a new conceptual meaning to a familiar word, without substantially changing its emotive meaning, and which is used with the conscious or unconscious purpose of changing the direction of people's interests. The words which mostly come in for definition of this kind are those which have a relatively vague 'conceptual' meaning but a very rich emotive meaning. People then seek, Stevenson says, to bestow on the word the qualities of their own choice. They steal, as it were, the good will (or bad will) which belongs to the word, and use it for their own ends. The conceptual content of the word may be so indefinite that it may manifest itself only in a feeling that at least one thing must not be left out in the new definition. Aristotle's treatment of the Greek word for happiness would be a case which Stevenson could use. There is little left of the 'conceptual' meaning, except that the word is felt to be necessarily associated somehow or another with pleasure, so that no definition would pass which did not accommodate the idea of pleasure. But apart from that, Aristotle makes few concessions and ends with the definition 'an activity of the soul in accordance with virtue', for which he makes use of the richly emotive word 'happiness' which everyone agrees is the thing to be aimed at. Examples could, of course, be multiplied. Stevenson is very careful to point out that the use of persuasive definitions is only one among many possible ways in which people may seek to influence other people and to change their interests. His contention is only that it is one of the most important methods in philosophical contexts, and this partly because it has so often been employed unknowingly. But if one's attention is drawn to the nature of persuasive definitions, it may become clear what ethical disputes are, and to what extent empirical methods are relevant in settling them. It will be worth while to take one further example to illustrate this point. This time the example is one which Stevenson himself uses. He considers the possible definitions of the word 'just'. He first envisages two men discussing the meaning of 'just' who agree that any law is just which leads to consequences A and B. If they do agree upon this, then trying to find out whether a particular law is just or not will be simply a matter of finding out if A and B do occur in consequence of it. Stevenson speaks as though this investigation is certain to be wholly empirical; and for the sake of formal presentation of his case I suppose this is justified. But in fact it is very unlikely that the supposed consequences A and B will be described in purely factual terms; they are far more likely themselves to be evaluated. And furthermore, dispute may well arise about whether, granted that both A and B occur, they are properly to be described as the consequences of the law under discussion. This is hardly a *straight* matter of fact, but itself involves a certain assessment of the situation. However, Stevenson wants a case which is supposed to be capable of being settled by appeal to the facts alone, since he wants to contrast this with a case where the two disputants disagree about the definition of justice in the following way: one of them says that a law is just if consequences A and B follow from it, the other says it is just only if consequences B and C follow from it. They may agree in the end that if B follows from it they can both call it just; but it is more likely that they will continue to dispute, not about whether C does or does not follow from the law, but whether the law is just. This kind of disagreement, then, turns into a genuine disagreement in interest, in which one party wishes to *recommend* laws whose consequences are A and B, while the other prefers laws whose consequences combine C with B. Even if they find out that it is wrong to say that the particular law does lead to C, while it is true that it leads to A and B, they may still argue about the justice of the law, even though 'conceptually speaking they have located no point of disagreement'. This disagreement is of the kind that no empirical method will be capable of solving. In analysing the meaning of such ethical terms as 'just', Stevenson suggests that it will usually be necessary to expose what factual elements are, in any given use of the word, being incorporated into its meaning. That is to say, at the beginning of any discussion of justice, for instance, or of generosity, or any other relatively specific ethical term, it will be necessary to set out clearly what definitions of these terms are being assumed. If this is done, the sting will be drawn from the persuasive definitions, since they will be revealed for what they are. These analyses he refers to as 'the second pattern of analysis'. He distinguishes them from the analysis which he recommended for the word 'good' in the first of his articles. There he suggested that the word 'good' had practically no factual content, but that its analysis was more or less of the form 'I like this. Like it as well' where nothing except interests were alluded to. At the end of the third article, he suggests that this first pattern of analysis is suitable for all highly generic ethical or aesthetic words, of which of course 'good' is the best example in both fields, while the second pattern will most probably be needed to deal with any more specific word in either field. But he also suggests that the desirability of using one pattern or the other cannot be laid down in advance of any particular argument.

It can now perhaps be seen in what ways Stevenson developed and improved upon the doctrine sketched in *The Meaning of Meaning* and, with more force, in *Language, Truth and Logic*. The main improvement was the distinction between those ethical terms which he thought had practically no factual or conceptual content, and those which he thought had at least some. His first pattern of analysis, thought to be sufficient for 'good', does not essentially differ from Ayer's. It is the same view of the meaning of 'good' which we noticed was to be found in Berkeley. Even here Stevenson did embark on the valuable distinction between the dynamic *use of* the word and its more permanent emotive meaning. And he did, as I pointed out above, insist more upon the truly emotive function of the word, as against its supposed expressive function, than Ayer had. This, too, seems to me to be an improvement. In the second pattern of analysis, on the other hand, he introduces far more scope for the complexity of moral discourse than had hitherto been allowed for in the theory. Even the recognition that 'good' is not the only ethical word in the English language, and that words like 'just' merit discussion as well is enlightened, though it is apparently a lesson which needs to be learned over and over again. Finally, in the discussion of persuasive definitions, Stevenson makes clearly explicit not only his reasons, but the reasons which really weighed with Ayer for rejecting any form of naturalism. Ayer used a logical argument similar to Moore's against any naturalistic definition of ethical terms. Stevenson on the other hand suggests that any such definition will be a cheat. For it will claim to give a total account of a word in terms of some empirically verifiable characteristics, while surreptitiously leaving untouched the emotive content of that word. For instance, if I claim to define 'good' as 'more evolved', a supposedly naturalistic or empirical epithet, although I may state that 'good' means *nothing more than* 'more evolved' I shall in so doing be disingenuous. For even if the factual content of the words were the same, still there is more in 'good' than there is in 'more evolved', namely the emotive meaning. My definition is therefore persuasive, for I have taken over the emotive content of 'good', and if anyone were tempted to accept my definition of 'good' and substitute 'more evolved' for 'good' in every case, they would either be treating 'good' in a new way, or importing into 'more evolved' an emotive sense which did not originally attach to it. Moore recognized that from every naturalistic definition of 'good' some crucial element which belonged *only* to 'good' was left out. Stevenson agrees with this and says that the crucial element in question is the emotive content of 'good'. Wherever Moore would have said that there was a case of the naturalistic

fallacy, a wrong attempt to define 'good', which was indefinable, there Stevenson would point to a case of 'persuasive
definition'. This insistence that ethics cannot be translated into
non-ethical language, that every attempt to do so is a cheat, is
the most fundamental principle of the emotive theory. As I
have suggested already, the subsequent history of moral philosophy in England reveals philosophers as almost obsessively
concerned with the details of this anti-naturalistic campaign.
Sometimes it may seem that the doctrines of the emotive theory
are almost too obvious to be worth such serious and long-
drawn-out investigation. But the feeling that they are obvious is
largely due to the extreme patience and lucidity with which
Stevenson presented them.

In 1945, Stevenson published a book called *Ethics and Language* which for some years became the bible of the emotive
theory. In some ways, however, the earlier articles which are
incorporated more or less in full into the book, are more interesting. They are certainly very much more readable. The book
seems to me to suffer from inflation and from a resulting
failure of impact, compared with the articles. It is as if Stevenson had become over self-conscious about methodology and
there is a good deal of reflexive commenting upon his own pro-
cedures, which add little or nothing to the actual ethical theory.
The book turns upon the distinction which was already contained in the articles between the 'first pattern of analysis' of
ethical terms, in which little or nothing is involved except the
laying bare of the interests or feelings expressed, and the 'second
pattern' in the course of which the 'conceptual content' of the
terms have also to be clearly stated. But I do not intend to say
any more about this, or indeed to discuss the book at all. Instead
I want to look a little more closely at the history of the theory
before Stevenson. For not only was he influenced by the early
Wittgenstein, and the logical positivists, as Ayer was, but, in
addition, he acknowledges a considerable debt to the American
philosophers Dewey and Ralph Barton Perry. In order therefore
to make the history of moral philosophy anything like complete
it is necessary to take into account, however briefly, the work of
these philosophers.

Dewey was, broadly speaking, a pragmatist. His influence on

American philosophy has been considerable, though I think he has never exported very well. There are several of his writings which are concerned with ethics, and in particular with the problem of how to distinguish ethical from non-ethical terms. The earlier pragmatists, in particular William James, had held that all possible different kinds of value judgements were judgements of means to ends. To say that anything of any kind was good was to say that it was both fitted for some special purpose, and that it was conducive to the general end of action, namely 'the good'. But this account was extended to cover not only value judgements ordinarily so called, but all judgements whatever. For 'true' and 'real' were also to be viewed as parts of 'the good'; they were each a particular kind of satisfaction of desire. Therefore any fact whatever would be judged by the same standard. If I state that something is red, or if I state that it is good, what I say will be allowed to be true if regarding it as red or regarding it as good are conducive to the satisfaction of desires of different kinds. Thus the distinction between judgements of value and judgements of fact has been obliterated. (The fullest statement of this view is perhaps to be found in William James's *Philosophical Conceptions and Practical Results* published in 1898.[1]) Dewey was seeking to reintroduce this very distinction.

But even Stevenson is bound to admit that 'Dewey does not always write in a way that lends itself to one and only one interpretation', and therefore I cannot hope to do more than state what I believe his views to have been without claiming any kind of finality of interpretation. In a book entitled *The Quest for Certainty*, which was published in 1929,[2] Dewey made a distinction between those statements which serve to 'give mere reports' and those which serve to 'make judgements as to the importance of bringing a fact into existence; or if it is already there of sustaining it in existence'.

A judgement [he says] about what is to be desired and enjoyed is . . . a claim on future action; it possesses a *de jure* and not merely *de facto* quality. . . . It is in effect a judgement that the thing 'will do'. It involves a prediction; it contemplates a future in which the thing

[1] Berkeley, Calif., 1898.
[2] Minton, Balch, N.Y., 1929; G. Allen & Unwin, London, 1930.

will continue to serve; it *will* do. It asserts a consequence that the thing will actively institute; it will *do*.

Part of the trouble with this passage is undoubtedly the style, which seems to owe more to Henry than to William James. But the main point may be made as follows: There is a kind of prediction involved in giving a scientific description of a thing, namely that the thing will continue to behave in a certain way and that we shall reach the truth about it if we describe it in a certain way. The fact that the truth, even about matters of science, is partially relative to our purposes need not here be taken into account. The prediction involved in a judgement upon the value of a thing is of a different kind. It is the prediction that the thing in question will become an end (or will become something to be avoided), and will therefore direct human activity in the future. An ethical judgement, that is, is a judgement that the speaker likes an object and that he regards it as fit to be liked in future, by himself and other people. 'Moral science,' Dewey says (and he presumably means the knowledge of what things are good and what are bad), 'is not something with a separate province. It is physical, biological and historic knowledge placed in a human context where it will illuminate and guide the activities of men.' Thus the distinction between judgements of value and judgements of fact, while it has very properly been reintroduced, is not regarded as a sharp or absolute one. Both types of judgement involve predictions, but in describing their objects in different terms they concentrate upon different aspects of the future to predict; they concern themselves with different human purposes. While scientific knowledge does in fact illuminate and guide the activities of men, ethical knowledge is specifically intended to do this and nothing else. Good, sober ethical judgements, therefore, will be those made with an eye to the consequences of actions which it is thought useful and sensible to pursue. The actions which are likely to have most of these desirable consequences will be those for which terms of praise will be reserved.

Stevenson, while acknowledging his debt to Dewey, and agreeing with him in regarding ethical judgements as particularly intended to redirect attitudes, criticizes him for 'absorbing emotive meaning into predictive suggestion'. He thinks it is odd that Dewey, 'whose views so readily suggest a quasi-imperative element in ethics . . . should have been so neglectful of emotive meaning'. He further criticizes him for over-emphasizing, as a consequence of this neglect, the degree to which empirical methods would be conclusive in setting ethical disputes. To take this second criticism first, it does not seem to me true to say that Dewey was committed to the belief that empirical methods *alone* could settle ethical arguments. No doubt he did think that the most important feature in any ethical judgement was the regard which such judgements necessarily paid to the consequences of the action judged. But part of the point of his theory, as I understand it, is that not only are consequences predicted, to which, of course, empirical investigation is relevant, but these consequences are also themselves assessed; and to assess them is to adopt a certain attitude towards them which is not a matter of empirical investigation. One quotation, again from *The Quest for Certainty*, may serve to show that this is his view: 'Men *like* some of the consequences and *dislike* others. Henceforth . . . attaining or averting similar consequences are aims or ends. These consequences constitute the meaning and value of an activity as it comes under deliberation.' Not only has one to determine what the consequences of an action will be; one has also to assess them. This at least seems clear. I regard this part of Stevenson's criticism, therefore, as misplaced. As for his general complaint that Dewey unduly neglects emotive meaning, my sympathies here again are rather with Dewey. Stevenson suggests one reason why this neglect may have come about, namely that Dewey concerns himself mainly with describing and analysing situations of *choice*. He constantly tries to set out the considerations which weigh with someone who is trying to decide what he should do, and to analyse the meaning of the terms in which such a man would describe his choice. Stevenson, on the other hand, is all the time primarily concerned with arguments between two people about how to judge some situation, perhaps an action of someone else. This difference may seem trivial, but I think it is not without importance. The obsession which the emotive theorists manifest with the meaning of ethical words, tends to direct their attention more and more to the process of describing things. The difference between ethical and non-ethical terms can be most clearly indicated in the difference between describing something factually, 'descriptively', and describing it emotively, in such a way as to influence people's attitudes towards it. The logical positivists' insistence that ethical language was strictly meaningless derived from the fact that a non-ethical *description* could be empirically checked, while an ethical one could not. The world is regarded as totally composed of facts, of happenings and being so, which can be properly described in one and only one way. All language which obscures the bare structure of these facts is at best misleading. Ethical words are marked off as failed descriptions; and in order to bring out this character in them, it is necessary always to represent them as being used quasi-descriptively—that is to denominate things good or bad. Only so can the real distinction between 'good' and 'red' be brought out. This, therefore, leads to these philosophers' interest in how *I* would describe *your* action; their world seems peopled with judges or schoolmasters, perpetually assessing and grading the conduct of others. Of course they would say that whatever they claim of these pseudo-descriptions could be applied *mutatis mutandis* to the judgements one makes about one's own future conduct, that is to one's own inner debates about what to do. But they seldom make the necessary changes, and we remain short of examples. In any case, it is far from clear that the process of deciding what to do *is* exactly like the process of judging somebody else's actions.

This is one reason, then, which Stevenson himself calls attention to, which may have influenced Dewey to neglect the emotive or imperative force of ethical words. It is less easy to think of someone perpetually trying to influence his own tastes, judgements, and actions by applying the pressure of emotive language than it is to think of someone's doing this for somebody else. The other reason why Dewey may have failed, in Stevenson's view, to pay enough attention to the emotive meaning of ethical terms is that perhaps he did not actually think it important enough. Stevenson himself suggests that perhaps his 'seeming omission of emotive meaning is rather a failure to abstract it out and emphasize it'. He can hardly have been unaware that some words have emotive overtones as well as

meaning in the normal sense. He was certainly aware that sometimes evaluative words may be used as something like expressions of feeling. (There is a chapter called 'Value Expressions as
Ejaculatory' in *Theory of Valuation*.[1]) But this feature of ethical
terms may not have seemed to be the central feature which
distinguished ethical from non-ethical terms. Of course, if his
kind of theory were correct, if it were true that in applying an
ethical epithet to something you were saying that it was or was
not an end which people would adopt, it would doubtless follow
that ethical language would acquire emotive overtones, or even
what might be described as a relatively permanent emotive
meaning; but this part of the meaning would be based on the
other, and therefore to call attention to the emotive meaning
alone would not be to give a sufficient analysis of an ethical
term. Stevenson himself is of course perfectly aware of this,
and, especially in his second pattern analysis, he insists that the
emotive and the non-emotive elements of the meaning are
present together. But he does not regard the emotive element as
secondary and derivative, as I conceive that Dewey would. In
this respect, I must confess once more to the belief that Dewey is
right.

About Perry, I must be even briefer. His main work on
ethics is entitled *General Theory of Value*.[2] He uses the word
'interest' (which has already appeared in the above discussion of
Stevenson, who takes the word over from him) to cover all
attitudes of liking, disliking, hating, admiring, and so on. His
theory is very like that ascribed by Ayer to Hume; that is, he
says that to judge that something is good is the same as to judge
that most people have a favourable interest in it. He is, of
course, criticized by Stevenson for in fact producing 'approved
of by everyone' as a definition of 'good'; and this is a typical
example, on Stevenson's theory, of a persuasive definition. He is,
that is to say, a naturalist in ethics. He takes extremely seriously
the consequence of his definition of 'good' that 'better' must
necessarily mean 'liked by more people' and 'worse' must mean
'disliked by more people'. Stevenson quotes the following state-

[1] University of Chicago Press, 1939.
[2] Longmans, N.Y., 1926; Harvard University Press, Cambridge,
Mass., 1950.

ment, 'An object which is loathed by L and M is worse, other things being equal, than an object which is loathed only by L or only by M.' He does, it must be admitted, introduce various other criteria by which to distinguish the better from the worse, but they are all of them connected with interests, though the way of judging is not always simply numerical as the above passage suggests. There are, for instance, degrees of intensity of dislike, and degrees of inclusiveness of dislike. But what he has produced is a very elaborate hedonistic calculus to help us judge between different things. The difference between his calculus and Bentham's is that his is much harder to apply, since we are asked to weigh up not the pleasure or pain which follows in consequence of a certain type of act, but the pleasure or pain caused in the contemplation of it. For 'Theft is bad' is construed as meaning not 'Theft has consequences which are painful to this or that degree', but as 'Most people dislike theft a very great deal'. The very natural next question might seem to be 'Why do they dislike it so much?' and it might further be tempting to supply a utilitarian answer to this question, in terms of the harm done by theft. But it is this further question and answer which Perry will not accept as relevant (and which, in spite of Ayer, Hume certainly would have accepted). It is mainly because of his insistence on stopping his analysis at just this point that Perry can be said to be influential upon, or at any rate typical of, the emotivist moral philosophers.

The influence of Dewey and Perry on Stevenson was undoubtedly, as he himself says, considerable; and therefore through Stevenson they indirectly influenced the emotivist theory in England as well. But far more important for the *development* of the theory was the pervasive influence of the later Wittgenstein. It is difficult to be precise on this matter, and in any case this is not the place to attempt any full account of the general revolution in the philosophical outlook for which he was responsible, and of which the changed approach to moral philosophy formed a part. But perhaps the most significant feature of the revolution for present purposes may roughly be said to be this: it no longer seemed adequate simply to state what a certain important philosophical concept really was, or how it was to be delimited. Instead, the actual and possible occurrences of the concept in thought had to be investigated; actual and possible languages in which the concept was embedded had to be described. The only way to solve philosophical problems which cluster round some concepts particularly, is to describe in the greatest possible detail the uses which we actually make or might make of them. In so doing we may come to see how we were previously bewildered, and where the preconceptions came from out of which, typically, philosophical problems arise. The application of this treatment to ethical concepts is obvious. The very opposite treatment of them to Wittgenstein's is perhaps that of Prichard, who, though he made some distinctions in meaning with precision, would suddenly insist, without evidence or investigation, that the *real* or *central* meaning of a word was such and such. His treatment of the concept of action, which I quoted in the last chapter, would do as a clear instance of this method; it will be remembered that 'we had in the end to allow' that *really* we meant by 'action' 'bringing about some new state of affairs'. His treatment of what he conceived to be the peculiar and distinct meaning of 'good' is another example. 'Good', he said, just *is* applicable to states of affairs, and only to states of affairs. When someone pointed out that as a child he had often been called a good boy by his Nanny, Prichard, after some thought, austerely replied that the Nanny had been confused. Again, the whole of *Principia Ethica* rests on exactly the assumptions which Wittgenstein aimed to combat. Moore not only thought that he could distinguish ethical from non-ethical uses of 'good' in one sentence, and thereafter leave the non-ethical uses entirely out of account, but he also thought that, within the sphere of the ethical, it was possible, just by inspection, to perceive that 'good' was indefinable, and that it applied uniquely to some things, and not at all to others. In Stevenson's article in *Mind*, for the first time, there are traces of a determination really to find out how ethical words such as 'good' are in fact used. (It is largely because the impact of Wittgenstein upon Stevenson is more clearly revealed in these articles that they are so much more interesting than his book.) It is no longer considered enough just to *state* that 'good' is indefinable, or that it is an expression of a favourable feeling. Examples are used to bring out the complexity of the kinds of disagreement which might actually occur between people about whether something was good or not; and this complexity is reflected especially in Stevenson's 'second pattern' analyses of ethical terms, where it is admitted that a great number of factual considerations may be relevant to determining whether an action is, for instance, an act of generosity or not, but that none of these factual considerations will determine us by themselves to apply a favourable epithet like 'generous', unless we wish also to express our approval, and to urge others to share it. Stevenson's insistence that the most he can give is patterns or models of analyses of such terms is itself an example of the refusal to accept any *single* analysis, derived from 'thinking out the matter clearly' as Prichard would have us do. In Stevenson's articles there is not only the recognition that 'goodness' is a very complex concept, and 'good' a word which we may have to see in use before we can understand it, but there is even, for the first time, the suggestion that 'good' is not the only interesting ethical term. Both these insights appear to be at least partially the result of the influence of Wittgenstein.

5

After the Emotivists

BECAUSE OF THE WAR, Stevenson's book was not generally available in England until 1947. It was then eagerly read and discussed. By this time the influence of Wittgenstein upon English philosophy, and particularly philosophy in Oxford, was extremely strong, although the *Philosophical Investigations* had not yet been published. Roughly speaking, the greatest part of moral philosophy in England for the next ten years may be divided into two: the first part being in a sense the continuation of the work of Ayer and Stevenson, modified by an increase in subtlety and, sometimes, in sensitivity to the actual use of language; the second part being perhaps more directly influenced by Wittgenstein. This second part I shall refer to as moral psychology, or the psychology of action, and I shall discuss it in the next chapter. In this chapter I shall try to deal with the first of my rough divisions, and I must start with two preliminary apologies. In the first place, it is obvious that in dividing up the moral philosophy of the last ten years in this crude way, I am leaving out a great deal. What I shall discuss is not necessarily the best moral philosophy that has been written during that time. My contention is only that it is in the main stream, for good or ill. Secondly, it may be thought odd to lump such authors as Hare and Urmson under the general heading of continuers of the work of Ayer and Stevenson, particularly as there is no single writer on moral philosophy of this decade that I can think of who does not repudiate emotivism. Of course I do not wish to call them emotivists; and I admit that there are great differences between their doctrines and the crude doctrines of the logical positivists. But still they have far more in common with Ayer than with, for instance, Moore, and there is some justification, therefore, in treating the present chapter as a kind of continuation of the last. It is futile to speculate too much about what philosophers will be read in a hundred years' time. But my guess is that posterity will not distinguish these authors very carefully one from the other. My second apology, then, is for guessing in this rash way and acting on my guess.

The emotivists insisted, like Moore, that ethics was nonnatural. From no set of ordinary empirical statements could you derive, by any means, a single ethical statement. There was a permanent and all-important gulf between fact-stating statements and the statements of ethics. This was one of the foundations of their doctrine. The second and equally important foundation was that ethical statements were non-descriptive. They were not, in fact, statements in the proper sense of the word. They were specially designed to do something other than to convey information. These two foundations are not questioned by the authors I wish now to consider. The difference between them and Stevenson lies in the precise function which they suppose ethical statements to have. One of the clearest and most straightforward statements of this kind of view is to be found in an article by Urmson, published in *Mind* in 1950, and entitled 'On Grading'.[1] Urmson confines himself to discussing the word 'good', among ethical words, and expressly states that his explanation does not extend to cover the words 'right' or 'ought', though it is fairly easy to see how, with suitable modifications, these words too could be accommodated. But the main part of his article is not concerned particularly with ethics at all, but with the general features of that particular use of language which he marks off as the grading use. Just as, in Stevenson's book, ethical language was treated as a sub-class of emotive language in general, so here ethical grading, the denomination of things morally good or morally bad, is regarded as a sub-class of grading in general.

Grading is regarded as an *activity*, something which may either be done physically, by moving things into piles, or verbally, by classing things in order of merit. Sometimes grading is

[1] *Mind*, Volume LIX, pp. 145 *sqq.*

spoken of as though it were a possible function of sentences, not of people, but this is an understandable shift. Urmson starts by considering the grading of apples according to the standards laid down by the Ministry of Agriculture. The apples are classified as super, extra fancy, fancy, domestic, and so on, down the scale. The first thing which he notices about the activity of grading these apples is that there are criteria for placing the apples in their different classes which can be precisely specified, and which are listed by the Ministry, under the title 'Definitions of Quality'. Secondly, he calls attention to the fact that an apprentice in sorting apples could learn to sort them into their various categories, by observing the distinguishing criteria for each class, without understanding that the categories in fact placed the apples in order of merit. Urmson says that it is doubtful whether this 'blind' sorting of apples should properly be called grading or not, but decides that it probably should not. He therefore lays it down as one of the conditions necessary for proper grading, that the grader should know what he is doing. He next makes two points which have obvious importance in the application of the general description of grading to ethical cases. He warns us against two opposite mistakes. The first is to suppose that the presence in a thing of those qualities which serve as grading criteria *entails* the applicability of the grading label. The second is to suppose that the applicability of the grading label to an object shows that the object has some *further* property, over and above those properties which served as criteria for placing it in this class or in that. The first warning can clearly be seen to be a generalized warning against naturalism. We must never think that saying that an object has any particular set of characteristics *comes to the same as* saying that it has some ethical property, such as goodness; the second warning is against intuitionism, the supposition that ethical properties are properties over and above natural properties, which may be the ground or foundation for them, but can never be identified with them. The point is that grading labels are not the names of properties or qualities at all. They simply mark the presence of this unique and irreducible *activity*, grading, which cannot be identified with describing in any terms at all, natural or non-natural. The theory is that to say of someone that he is first class is not to describe him; it is to do something to him, namely place him in the first class. Urmson goes on rather briefly to apply his general remarks on grading to the case of ethics. Although he remarks in passing that words like 'brave' and 'cowardly' are grading labels, he confines his attention in the main to the ethical use of the word 'good', though he admits that there are difficulties inherent in discussion of 'good' due to what he calls its vagueness, which I would prefer to call its generality. The important point in the analogy between the ethical and the non-ethical cases is that in both cases, if we grade something, there must exist criteria in accordance with which we are grading it. Urmson goes so far as to say that we should be able to state what these criteria are, and that stating the criteria will be stating what moral standards we adopt. He does not say anything much about where we get these criteria from, nor why we accept as criteria for moral excellence one set of characteristics rather than another. This might well seem to be a matter of great importance, but it is not the subject of this particular article. The consequence of its omission, however, is a certain artificiality in the concept of sets of criteria, or moral standards. Urmson speaks as though we all of us had just one moral standard, and that in the course of arguing about the goodness or badness of something, we could, if need be, trot out a complete set of criteria. This artificiality is of course partly due to the original analogy between moral grading and the grading of apples according to some previously laid down set of rules, which could be discovered by looking them up in the Ministry's hand-out.

The weakness of the analogy comes out most clearly in the brief discussion at the end of the article about moral disagreements. Here Urmson's views are very close to Stevenson's, whose second pattern of analysis he does, rather grudgingly, refer to. Urmson is obliged to hold that, just as when grading apples according to different standards, one could not use any of the grading labels from either list in order to judge which *set of standards* was the best, so with ethics, if it turns out that two people have different moral standards, it is impossible to use moral terms derived from the vocabulary of either of them in order to adjudicate between the standards. He thinks that there may be moral disagreements of a less fundamental kind than this, as where, for instance, two people, though they adopt the same moral standards, may differ about the precise application of one of the set of criteria in a difficult case. But he thinks that when the ultimate disagreement has been revealed, namely a difference in *what criteria are being used*, then no *moral* arbitration between the parties is possible, nor, if they are honest, will they be entitled to call each other's view bad or immoral. This seems to me to be exceedingly implausible; and I think that here again the absurdity lies in the suggestion that there is a finite list of moral criteria, which together make up our moral code, the whole of which could, if necessary, be stated. If this were possible, and if two such codes were then laid side by side and seen to be different from one another, it might indeed, as Urmson suggests, be possible to characterize one only as more enlightened than the other, and not as more morally admirable. For the question might then reasonably be raised, 'morally admirable according to which code?' But it is only the persuasive force of the Ministry of Agriculture's finite set of Definitions of Quality, together perhaps with a lurking analogy with legal codes, which could make us think even for a moment that moral codes were like this. It would be perfectly extraordinary if anyone could in fact set out a complete list of all the characteristics which he proposed to use for judging things morally good or bad. And even if he succeeded in listing all the things he could think of which went to make up his moral code, and if he found some other moral code which differed from his own, he would not be very likely just to notice the fact that the other code was different and that therefore the uses of such words as 'good' and 'bad' were ambiguous, according to which code was being employed. This kind of liberality may be all very well in the context of grading apples. No one would do more than express surprise if he came across persons who graded apples as extra fancy on the grounds that they had maggots. But it seems to be one of the peculiar marks of moral beliefs that they cannot be so dispassionately compared. Urmson tries, by the help of his analogy, to make us think that there is some *logical* absurdity in picking a word from our moral vocabulary of grading in order to grade a total set of moral criteria or a moral code.

But there is no logical reason against doing this. If there seems to be, it is because we have been misled into thinking of moral codes as finite statable sets of criteria. As a rule we do not know what our moral standards are till they are tested by some new real case. We do not come armed to the cases with the criteria in our hand, still less with *all* the criteria.

But it is unfair to expect more from a single article than we get from Urmson's. It is a clear statement of an analogy supposed to throw light on the function of our ethical language, and to show that this ethical language is irreducible to any other kind. I now want to mention two other longer statements of the same kind of views.

The first is to be found in Hare's book *The Language of Morals*, published in 1952. The same views are elaborated and given more content in his second book; but the two books[1] together amount to a single statement, for they are perfectly consistent. Hare starts by telling us that his intention is to write an introduction to ethics for beginners and to 'bring the beginner as directly as possible to grips with the fundamental problems of the subject'. But very soon these fundamental problems turn out to be the very same problems which exercised Ayer and Stevenson, namely the correct characterization of the language which we use in making ethical statements. Hare indeed describes his own first book as a logical study of the language of morals. His contention is, briefly, that ethical language is a sub-species of prescriptive language, that is to say, language which is particularly designed to suggest courses of action to people. Prescriptive language in general may be divided into two classes, the class of overt imperatives, and the class of evaluative words or sentences. When this division is applied to ethics, it seems that 'ought' and 'right' and 'you should' come into the first class, being genuine imperatives, according to Hare; while 'good', 'desirable', and so on come into the second. There is here, therefore, a slight advantage, so far, over Urmson's analogy, since all the commonly discussed ethical words can be accommodated as prescriptive. Hare further maintains that the imperative class of prescriptive language is in a sense fundamental, since value judgements, if they are action-guiding at all, that is

[1] R. M. Hare. *Freedom and Reason*. Oxford University Press, 1963.

if they are truly prescriptive, must be held to entail at least one imperative. Thus from the proposition 'This is a good chocolate', if the proposition is truly evaluative, it must be legitimate to infer 'Take it'; or, if this sounds too absurd, perhaps a more complicated imperative should be substituted, namely, 'If there is any question of taking a chocolate, other things being equal, take this one'. There does seem to me to be a danger here. Either the inference rule just stated will turn out to be tautological, since no use of 'good' will be counted as fully prescriptive unless the inference is possible; or, if more uses of 'good' are to count as prescriptive, then the inference will simply not be possible. That is to say, as so often happens with philosophical principles, there is the danger that the principle will turn out to be either uninteresting, because tautological, or false. I do not think that Hare means to restrict very severely the uses of 'good' which he would count as evaluative in the proper sense, or prescriptive; and therefore I think that his claim that one must always be able to infer an imperative from any such use is simply mistaken. It is not at all clear that from 'This is good' you can always infer 'Therefore choose it', even when all possible provisos about other things being equal have been made. However, this is the contention. Ethical language is a sub-class of prescriptive language, which is, all of it, either directly imperative, or logically related to an imperative. What, we are told in the second book, marks off ethical language from other prescriptions is that it has universal applications. 'Take it', in an ethical context, becomes 'Let everyone take it'.

A good part of Hare's book is taken up with arguments to show that logical relations such as entailment and inconsistency may hold between propositions in the imperative mood, as well as between those in the indicative mood; and that therefore to say that an argument contains an imperative is not to say that it is irrational or governed by no logical laws. We are, moreover, presented with yet another version of the argument against naturalism, in the form of a proof that from indicative premisses nothing but an indicative conclusion can be deduced.

A good deal more of the book is concerned with the relation I have already discussed between the two main types of prescriptive language, the evaluative and the imperative. This is illustrated with examples, involving the use of the words 'good' and 'ought'. But we are never really told by Hare, any more than we were by Urmson, by what test we decide whether a word or sentence is prescriptive or not (nor whether it is really words or sentences that he is interested in). This seems to be supposed to be self-evident. Urmson, in the same way, while insisting that grading was an irreducible activity, and that there was a whole number of words which generally or always functioned as grading labels, did not in the least help us to decide in any given particular cases whether what someone was doing was grading or not. Both Urmson and Hare make it easier for themselves to leave out this important part of the theory by choosing to talk about 'good', which no one would seriously deny was at least very often evaluative. But there are many less general words where it seems to me difficult to say off-hand whether they are evaluative or not, whether they are used to grade, or just to say things. Stevenson, of course, was guilty of the same fault, but to a lesser extent. For he admitted that almost any word *could* have an emotive force, and he did attempt to limit his inquiry to those words whose emotive force had become somehow part of their meaning. He even tried to lay down criteria, by which to test whether this was so or not, for any given word. This was not entirely successful, but at least it was something. Both Hare and Urmson seem to take it for granted that the merest beginner in the consideration of language can tell at a glance whether a word is prescriptive or not, whether it grades or does not grade.

It must be emphasized once again that neither Hare's book nor Urmson's article have any very direct connexion with ethics. They are both of them concerned to show the logical characteristics of a general type of function which language may have, and of which the ethical function is a sub-species. Hare's books *seem* to have more relevance to ethics than Urmson's article, because Hare himself incidentally lets fall some views about morals, which Urmson does not. For instance, Hare believes that all moral action is action according to some statable principle, and that the more morally grown-up we become, the less simple our principles are. He connects this thesis with the general thesis of the book, by referring to moral principles as general imperatives. For example, he says that 'it is part of our moral development' to turn principles such as 'never say what is false' 'from provisional principles into precise principles with the exceptions definitely laid down'. Thus, as we reach the stage of being morally grown-up we are supposed to approach the question of what we ought to do in any situation with this list of definite instructions, which have been made more and more definite (or rather, precise) over the years. Perhaps this is not so very far from Urmson's implied view too. For if we adopt the grading analogy for moral discourse, we are supposed, as we have seen, to approach the judgement of situations with a definite list of criteria according to which we are going to adjudicate them morally good or bad. In both cases there seems to be an almost ludicrous over-simplification of the actual methods we adopt in deciding what to do or how to live.

The last example of this kind of theory which I want to discuss is Nowell-Smith's. This is to be found in his book *Ethics* published in 1954. This is an altogether more ambitious and comprehensive book than Hare's, and my treatment of it will therefore be proportionately more inadequate. As a matter of fact a good deal of Nowell-Smith's book is devoted to the kind of subject which I have already referred to as the 'psychology of action'; this part of the book is therefore not relevant to the present chapter. But it should be noticed that my discussion of the parts of the book which are relevant may suggest that the whole book is a great deal thinner and less comprehensive than it is. Nowell-Smith has a very wide conception of what is properly a part of ethics, and in this way, if in no other, he is to be sharply distinguished from the writers I have so far discussed in this chapter and the last. But although his view of the subject matter of ethics appears to be wider, his statement of his own purpose sounds familiar. He says that he is trying to 'make clear the complicated connexions between such words as "good", "right", "ought", "choose", "duty", "desire", and "pleasure" '. The best thing about this list is that it is comparatively long. Even more familiar is the note sounded by the editorial foreword to Nowell-Smith's book; and this is not surprising since it was written by Ayer. He says:

There is a distinction, which is not always sufficiently marked, between the activity of a moralist, who sets out to elaborate a moral code, or to encourage its observance, and that of a moral philosopher, whose concern is not primarily to make moral judgements but to analyse their nature. Mr. Nowell-Smith writes as a moral philosopher. He shows how ethical statements are related to, and how they differ from statements of other types, and what are the criteria which are appropriate to them.

We have so far been offered a decent variety of answers to the question how ethical statements differ from statements of other types. We have been told that they are expressions of feeling, that they are designed both to express and to evoke the feelings of others, that they have the function of grading, that they are imperatives, or logically closely related to imperatives. Nowell-Smith does not favour any single simple solution to this problem. In the course of his exposition he has occasion to invent various technical terms, one of which is 'the Janus principle', namely the principle that any one statement or word may be expected to perform at least two functions on any one occasion of its use, and perhaps more than two. Thus, appealing to this principle, he rejects the views that ethical expressions are *just* imperative or *just* emotive, or that they have any other single unique function. But there are words, which can be listed, which characteristically have, among other functions, that of suggesting a suitable reaction to something. An example of such a word would be 'horrible', which suggests that the object so described is apt to call forth horror. Nowell-Smith calls these words 'A words', short for Aptness words, 'because they are words that indicate that an object has certain properties which are *apt* to arouse a certain emotion or range of emotions'. These A words are contrasted on the one hand with D words ('purely descriptive, according to the current distinction between descriptive and evaluative'), and on the other hand with G or Gerundive words, which suggest that an object has properties which *ought* to be regarded in a certain way. 'Praiseworthy' is an example of a G word. The distinction between A and G would not, I think, be supposed by Nowell-Smith to be hard and fast. It is simply that some words suggest a normal reaction, others a desired or required reaction. In his subsequent discussion of the first class of adjectives, those which suggest emotions, Nowell-Smith covers a good deal of the ground covered by Stevenson. He concludes that these words are used to give explanations and make predictions, not to give reasons. But their use is only proper if the user has in mind reasons of a certain sort which are not stated but contextually implied. Thus it will be proper to say of something that it is horrible only if I have reasons for saying it, among which will be that I dislike the thing in question. Nowell-Smith makes a good deal of use of the concept of 'oddity' or 'logical oddity' and I think that logical oddity is supposed to be the penalty we should pay if we used one of these emotive or A words *without* the normally relevant reasons being present, or, still more, if we used the word but denied the reason. Thus, if I insist both that something is horrible and that I like it, I think that Nowell-Smith would say that I had committed a logical oddity. Exception might be taken to the expression 'logically odd'. It is not, for one thing, very clear. It is supposed to characterize something less than contradiction, but akin to it. So far this is all right. One might at first be tempted to say I had contradicted myself if I said that something which I liked was horrible, and then one might reflect a bit and decide that after all it was less than a contradiction. But if so, then I do not quite see why we need any special name for the kind of surprising thing I am supposed to have said. There could be a number of different explanations of my saying it. I might simply mean that, though the thing was horrible by other people's standards, it was not so by mine. This would not count as a case of logical oddity, for Nowell-Smith would say that in this case I was not using 'horrible' as a truly A word—that is, I was using it descriptively. Or it might be that I really did feel ambivalent about the object; I both hated it and liked it. In this case I do not see why the oddness is particularly a matter of logic. It may be that my reactions are odd.

It is valuable, I am sure, to point out that between 'This is horrible' and 'I like this' there is a relation which is not that of contradiction. This is at least to suggest that the whole meaning of 'It is horrible' is not given by the translation 'I dislike this'. For 'I like this' and 'I dislike this' are, at least on the face of it, contradictory. And therefore 'This is horrible' must mean something different from 'I dislike this'. It is right to point this out. But only the very early pioneering emotivists would ever have maintained that 'This is horrible' did mean *only* 'I dislike this'. It was very soon common ground that all emotive words had *some* descriptive content, some more than others. I do not think that Nowell-Smith has made this point any clearer by introducing the notion of 'logical oddity' to be the name of what happens when the normal concomitance of descriptive and emotive meaning falls apart.

Nowell-Smith connects his Gerundive words with the possession in the user of them of a favourable attitude towards some relevant action or choice. Thus, if I say that something is right, I am using a Gerundive word and I may also be taken to have a favourable or 'pro' attitude to the doing of the thing in question. He maintains, however, that the connexion is not simple. A person's favourable attitudes, that is, his desires and interests and wishes, form a background without which he could not intelligibly use words like 'ought' and 'right' and 'duty' at all. But he might have all these favourable attitudes without having any concept of duty at all. Favourable attitudes, therefore, are in a sense prior to Gerundive words, and serve to explain them, just as the actual characteristics of things are in a sense prior to our feelings about them, and serve to explain our feelings. Thus both Aptness words and Gerundive words have to be explained in terms of something other than themselves.

These points need, as we have come to expect, have nothing to do with ethics specifically. They are perfectly general points about our use of language in all contexts of appraising, describing (in the real, non-philosophical, sense, in which I may describe things as ghastly or wonderful), advising, and choosing. But once again it is easy to see that they can be applied to specifically ethical language. 'Morally good' will function both as an Aptness word and as a Gerundive word. It will normally both suggest certain appropriate feelings, and suggest that the object so described is a fit object of choice. 'Good', Nowell-Smith says, is the Janus word *par excellence*. It will have at least these two functions in its proper moral use, and perhaps more. All moral words will be used, when properly used, in at least these two ways. They are not then descriptive words; they do not name properties. Nor are we told at all what things have the characteristics such that we should be justified in having pro feelings and pro attitudes towards them, in the context of morality or outside it. But there is one point for which one may be grateful to Nowell-Smith. He agrees with other philosophers of the twentieth century that the naturalistic fallacy is to be avoided; and he thinks of the naturalistic fallacy, as we should expect, as the mistake of supposing that evaluative words can be defined wholly in terms of non-evaluative or descriptive words. Further, he agrees that the reason why this inter-definition is not possible is that evaluative words are not used to describe at all but to do something different. But he does allow that the philosophers who have mostly been accused of committing the fallacy would not really have been very much shaken if it had been pointed out to them. They were not, and here I quote Nowell-Smith,

primarily interested in the question whether deontological words could be analysed in terms of 'merely empirical' or 'natural' concepts. They believed that, human beings being what they are, there are certain types of activity that are in fact satisfactory to them and that it is possible empirically to discover what these are. . . . They do not seem to have been mistaken in their basic assumptions that the language of obligation is intelligible only in connexion with the language of purpose and choice, that men choose to do what they do because they are what they are, and that moral theories which attempt to exclude all consideration of human nature as it is do not even begin to be moral theories.

There is surely good sense in this. We may agree that ethical language is different from non-ethical; even that evaluative language in general is different from, and cannot be derived from, non-evaluative language. But this does not mean that as a matter of fact what we value highly cannot be non-evaluatively described; nor even that no natural explanation can ever be forthcoming of why we value it as we do. Perhaps the fear of naturalism in ethics has had too firm a grip.

It can now perhaps be seen how the emotivism which started with the logical positivists developed. In the first instance, emotivism was a way out of what had come to seem like two alternative accounts of ethics, both unsatisfactory; namely, naturalistic ethics on the one hand, and intuitionism on the other. Naturalistic ethics in its most plausible form is utilitarianism, and in order to reject it the emotivists had to interpret it as a theory which stated that the whole meaning of the word 'good' could be given by some set of non-ethical words such as 'productive of pleasure'. If this had been true, ethical statements could have been translated into fact-stating terms, and would therefore have been admissible as real statements even by the positivists. But such a theory seemed to them false. One should perhaps notice, as I have suggested before, that what they criticize is a very much enfeebled version of utilitarianism. I do not think that any utilitarian would have been inclined to deny that 'good' had emotive force, or that it was an A word and a G word. And he might have, therefore, been perfectly prepared to agree that an actual translation of the word 'good' into something about pleasure might not work. But he would have said that his theory never depended for a moment on the possibility of such a translation. He was concerned to establish what things people thought were good, what things people adopted as ultimate ends; and if some ways of describing the ends had more emotive power than others, this would not disturb the theory. But in any case, the positivists were not concerned with questions such as what people actually adopt as their ends. They thought it was clear that scientifically verifiable statements could not include any ethical propositions, or evaluations of any kind, and therefore they rejected any claim to be able to incorporate evaluations indirectly, by means of a translation into the supposedly non-evaluative word 'pleasure', or any other non-evaluative word. They also, naturally, rejected the claims of the intuitionists to be able to apprehend certain non-scientific properties of things. Their alternative was to say that ethical and evaluative language was not informative at all, was not concerned with the properties of objects, whether scientific or metaphysical. Evaluative language was concerned to do something else, namely to express. I think the subsequent history of the theory, in all the various forms which we have looked at, shows an increased awareness of the complexity of language. At first there seemed to be a kind of triumph in the discovery that language could do anything at all except be used to convey information. Philosophers seemed so pleased to have found this out that they were content to use the word 'emotive' to cover a large number of quite different things which language could do. The most notorious example of this lack of precision is Ayer's initial failure seriously to distinguish between the functions of expressing feelings of one's own, and attempting to arouse the feelings of others. But even Stevenson, who went into the matter so much more thoroughly, and who was clearly under the influence of Wittgenstein, which might have made him cautious about lumping different functions of language together, was fairly vague in his directions for picking out emotive meaning, and for saying precisely what was covered by the term. Nowell-Smith, in contrast, is very much more cautious in putting things together, and more hesitant in claiming completeness. The trouble has always been, partly at least, that while some philosophers have been reasonably detailed in their particular accounts of evaluative language, they have never been at all clear about that with which they were contrasting it. They never even fixed on a wholly satisfactory word for that main body of linguistic use from which the evaluative use was being picked out. 'Non-evaluative' is of course the safest and least harmful. 'Descriptive', as I have already suggested, seems to me the worst. 'Scientific' is perhaps the best, in the sense that the old positivistic contrast comes out most clearly in it. I do not think that this failure is trivial. If a whole ethical theory is meant to turn on the fact that ethical language is somehow importantly to be distinguished from the rest of language, it may surely suggest that the distinction has not been exactly made, if there are not satisfactory ways of referring to *both* sides of the distinction. To mark ethical language off simply from 'the rest' is to say too little. There might be too many ways in which it was different, and 'the rest' might be too internally various. But even to speak of *ethical* language being marked off is perhaps to go too far. For one thing which is common to all the philosophers who have been considered in this chapter and the last is that they were primarily discussing not ethics but evaluation in general. Nothing that they said applied more properly to ethics than to horticulture or fat-stock breeding. Any situation in which assessments and judgements have to be made was distinguished from the situations in which plain statement goes on. But the trouble is that we assess and evaluate practically all the time. Perhaps what prevented them from thinking of a useful description of the supposedly non-evaluative uses of language was that there are practically none of them. In any case the extremely frequent occurrence of evaluation in some form or another may well make us feel, when we come to the end of reading these theories, that we still need to be told something a bit more specific about ethics in particular, as opposed to evaluation in general. All the models and analogies to illuminate ethical language have the air of being preliminary clearings of the ground. We may naturally feel disappointed that, when the ground is cleared, nothing seems to happen.

good point!

6
Moral Psychology

In the last chapter I roughly divided contemporary moral philosophy into two parts, one of which was labelled the psychology of action. It is now time to turn to this second division of the subject. But at the outset, a further sub-division seems convenient. There has never been a time when moral philosophers have not concerned themselves with the subject of free will, and the present century is no exception. I want first of all to say something about the course which this traditional discussion has taken in the last ten years or so, and then to consider the more strictly psychological questions which have in many cases seemed to be connected with the traditional problem or even to arise out of it.

Some recent discussions of the freedom of the will have started from Moore's treatment of the subject, in his book called *Ethics*. Moore presented the issue between determinists and libertarians, and his possible solution of the difficulty, in the following way:

Those who hold that we *have* Free Will, think themselves bound to maintain that acts of will sometimes have *no* cause, and those who hold that everything is caused think that this proves completely that we have not Free Will. But in fact it is extremely doubtful whether Free Will is at all inconsistent with the principle that everything is caused. Whether it is or not, all depends on a very difficult question as to the meaning of the word 'could'.

He then goes on to explain that the crucial expression in the discussion of free choice is 'He could have done otherwise', since if anyone holds that a man could not have done otherwise than he did, or could not help acting as he did, then the man is not held to be fully responsible for his act, he is not blamed for it, nor praised for it, and it ceases to be an act to which moral predicates are properly applied. This is the contention of both determinists and libertarians alike. And so the question is whether it is ever the case that a man *could* have acted otherwise than he did. Moore says that in the phrase 'I could have done otherwise', 'I could' means 'I would if I had chosen'; and he goes on to say:

For my part I must confess that I cannot feel certain that this may not be *all* that we mean and understand by the assertion that we have free will; so that those who deny that we have it are really denying . . . that we ever *should* have acted differently even if we had willed differently.

And again,

It is . . . quite certain (1) that we often should have acted differently if we had chosen to; (2) that similarly we often should have chosen differently if we had chosen so to choose; and (3) that it was almost always *possible* that we should have chosen differently in the sense that no one could know for certain that we should *not* so choose. All these three things are facts, and all of them are quite consistent with the principles of causality.

Moore, characteristically, did not present his solution to the problem as certainly correct; but he was clearly very much inclined towards it. According to this view, then, to say that men have free will is to say that they do choose to perform actions which they need not perform. To say this is the same as to say that there are cases in which a man could have acted otherwise than he did. To say this, again, means the same as to say that he *would have acted differently if he had chosen to*. And if it is objected that after all a man *could not have chosen* differently, Moore's answer is that this is just untrue. There is a perfectly good sense of 'possible' in which it was possible, before the choice was made, either that he would choose as he did, or that he would choose some other way. An observer of the man would not have been able to rule either out as impossible; and this is what is meant by saying it was possible that he could have

chosen either of the two things. The essential point of this solution to the problem is that it effects a reconciliation between
the determinists and the libertarians by showing that when we
speak of freely chosen actions, what we actually mean is something quite precise, which can be precisely shown not to entail
an absence of causation. There is no need for the libertarian to
try to maintain that there are some uncaused events, namely
human choices; he can be granted that choices are really free,
once it has been shown to him what he and other people actually
mean when they speak of a free choice.

Broadly speaking, there have been two closely interconnected
ways of proceeding with the attempt to reinforce and supple-
ment Moore's initial presentation of the case, and to remove
the hesitations which he still felt about his reconciliation of the
determinists with the libertarians. On the one hand, Moore's
own analysis of the meaning of 'could have acted otherwise' has
been taken up, and its expansion into 'would have acted otherwise if . . .' has been further elaborated. I shall come back to
this development in a moment. On the other hand, further consideration has been given to the question what we do actually
mean when we speak of an act as free in general. The conclusion
of these second investigations has been that by a freely chosen
act is intended an act which a man was not compelled, in any
recognized way, to perform. That is to say, the natural opposite
of 'free' is not 'caused' but 'compelled' or some similar word.
Thus the supposed inconsistency between freedom of choice
and universal causation is shown to be non-existent since
'freely chosen' and 'caused' do not rule one another out. Hume
offered a solution to the problem on these lines and, still earlier,
so did Hobbes. There is nothing new, therefore, in the actual
attempt at reconciliation. But the methods of effecting the reconciliation have become more subtle and more precise. Furthermore, a great deal that is interesting in itself has come to
light in the course of this kind of examination of the concept of
free or voluntary action. Not all the discussions, indeed perhaps
not any of them, have been as bald and crude as what I have
said may suggest. For instance in the *Proceedings of the Aristotelian Society* for 1948, Professor H. L. A. Hart published an
article entitled 'The Ascription of Responsibility and Rights',

in which he discussed the concept of responsibility from the legal point of view, and here the many possible opposites of 'voluntary', as applied to actions, were brought out and the whole nature of the concept of responsibility clarified in an important way. Further light was thrown, though less directly, on the concept of freedom by Hart and Honoré's book *Causation in the Law*.[1] Such work as this has not been directed specifically to solving the traditional problem of the freedom of the will, but more generally to clarifying the notions of 'act', 'free act', 'responsibility', and 'choice'. But this clarification has obvious relevance to the traditional problem.

Let us return now to the connexion between 'He acted freely' and 'He could have acted otherwise': Nowell-Smith's book, *Ethics*, contains a discussion of free will which has been influential, and which derives directly from Moore's. His contention is that we call those actions free (and we therefore may praise or blame them), which we believe that a man *could* have chosen not to perform. When we say that he could have chosen not to perform an action, we mean that the man *would* have chosen not to perform it *if* certain conditions had been different. Nowell-Smith's account thus goes beyond Moore's in that it brings into the actual meaning of 'could have acted otherwise' the concept of conditions—not just the condition 'if he had chosen' but other conditions not yet specified. The main part of the discussion is directed to showing that there are some conditions which we allow as excuses; that is to say, there are some cases where 'He would have acted otherwise if . . .' is filled up with a condition which we feel it would have been impossible to fulfil; and in this sort of case we do not believe that the man really could have acted otherwise, and therefore we do not hold that he acted freely, in acting as he did. But there are other cases where the conditions mentioned in the 'if' clause are not allowed to excuse the man for doing what he did. These are the cases where we feel that he was in some way responsible, not only for what he actually did, but for being subject to the conditions he was subject to. Thus we tend to think that a man did not act freely, let us say, in infecting our children with

[1] H. L. A. Hart and A. M. Honoré, *Causation in the Law*. Oxford University Press, 1959.

typhoid, if he really could not have known that he was a carrier of the disease. So if he says 'I would have avoided them if I had known', if we are prepared to allow that he could not have known, we are also prepared to allow that he could not have helped infecting the children. On the other hand, if he says, trying to get out of it, 'I could not help giving them typhoid because I am so forgetful. If I had been more careful I would have avoided the children', we do not allow this as an excuse. We hold the man responsible for what he did, because we hold him responsible for being so careless. Nowell-Smith on the whole presents it simply as a matter of fact that some conditions mentioned in the 'I would have if . . .' clause excuse a man, and others do not; and chief among those which do *not* are conditions relating to a man's moral character. Thus I am never going to be allowed to get away with lying by saying 'I would have done otherwise if I had not been a liar', and hoping you will think I can't help being a liar. But he also has one proposed explanation of the difference between the conditions to which we are subject. He thinks that those conditions are held to be within our power (and are therefore not allowed as excuses) which punishment will alter. This curiously back-to-front view has been mentioned already. It was first fully discussed by Stevenson, who thought that those actions were held to be free which emotive language could influence a man either to perform or to refrain from. Free will could therefore, according to him, be actually defined in terms of the emotive use of language—as that which characterized behaviour with respect to which emotive language was liable to be effective. I do not think this view has any great plausibility. At any rate neither Stevenson nor Nowell-Smith seems to have devised a satisfactory formula for expressing the connexion, if it exists, between free will and the possibility of influence by reprobation and punishment.

A more fundamental doubt about the solutions offered by Moore and Nowell-Smith remains to be expressed. In both theories the solution offered was a demonstration that free choice was compatible with universal causation on the grounds that 'He could have acted otherwise' meant the same as 'He would have acted otherwise if something had been the case' and it was then shown that one way or another the something might, often, have been the case. But if one does not accept the identity of meaning between 'He could have acted otherwise' and 'He would have acted otherwise if . . . had been the case' then the demonstration breaks down. Neither Moore nor Nowell-Smith offers a conclusive argument to justify the translations they propose. Moore notices the change from 'could have if I had chosen' to 'should have if I had chosen' but says that he makes the change 'in order to avoid a possible complication', which is not much of a justification (and we are not told what the possible complication was). Nowell-Smith produces an example to show that the expressions 'he could have' and 'he would have if' mean the same, but it is not convincing. He says:

It is logically odd to say 'Smith can run a mile, has had several opportunities, is passionately fond of running, has no . . . reason for not doing so, but never has done so'. And, if it is true that this is logically odd, it follows that 'can' is equivalent to 'will . . . if . . .' and 'could have' to 'would have if . . .'

We have already had occasion to regret the expression 'logically odd'. Here it certainly does little to advance the argument. It is difficult to know whether to agree or disagree with the application of the expression to the case of Smith's running, and therefore it is impossible to use its applicability even as a ground for suggesting identity of meaning, let alone as a proof. And on the face of it the two expressions do not, I think, seem to mean the same. In a lecture delivered to the British Academy in 1956, Professor J. L. Austin argued that neither Moore's nor Nowell-Smith's translation of 'he could have' was correct. It is not possible to summarize the argument, much of which was directed against specific points of detail in both Moore's and Nowell-Smith's discussions. But one distinction of the greatest importance was brought out, and that is the distinction between the so-called conditional or subjunctive use of 'he could have' and the indicative use. The indicative use of 'he could have' means 'he was able to', and this is different from 'he would have been able to, if something or other', and also different from 'he would have, if something or other'. It certainly seems that to say of someone that he *was able* to do something does not say anything at all about what he *would have done* in certain specific circumstances. Admittedly we may collect evidence about what people are able to do from what they have done in the past; but this still does not entitle us to say anything about what they would have done in the past or would do in the future under certain conditions. If this is true, then, as Austin suggests, the compatibility between freedom of choice and determinism may after all be still subject to doubt. The reconciliation was effected by treating 'he could have acted otherwise' (the phrase which, for the libertarians, must essentially be saved) as hypothetical, meaning 'he would have acted otherwise if things had been different'. But if this awkward phrase turns out not after all to submit to this treatment, then the question remains to be answered whether it is true that on any given occasion the agent really could have acted otherwise, that is, whether, categorically, he had at the time the ability or the power to do otherwise than he did.

Now if the determinists are right in saying that there must be some causal explanation possible for everything that a man does, it looks as if it cannot be true that when he does one thing he really at that time has the power to do something else, things being as they are. A genuine causal explanation cannot, of its very nature, leave this possibility open. If I explain that your bicycle tyre is flat because I stuck a tin-tack into it, although obviously I can allow that if things had been different the tyre would not have been flat, I cannot allow that, with things as they are, viz. the tyre being capable of puncture by a tin-tack and my having stuck the tin-tack into it, the tyre could be other than flat. If I left this open, I should have failed to give a causal explanation of the thing you wanted explained. It must be possible to justify a properly causal explanation by saying 'Whenever this happens, that happens,' and this is precisely what would *not* be possible if it were really open to a man, in a given set of circumstances, to choose to do either of two things. Therefore, since we do talk of people choosing, and talk as though they could have chosen what they did not in fact choose, it looks very much as if what we say, and what we feel we need to say, about people's conduct is incompatible with what the determinists claim. This is not of course to say which of us is

N.B

Why is it that empiricists insist on using a realist conception of causality in ethics + a phenomenalist one in epistemology + metaphysics?

right. Determinism might be true, even though if we accepted it we should have to alter the way we talk about human conduct.

If, as I believe, then, the attempts which have recently been made to reconcile our ordinary beliefs with determinism break down, however attractive they look at first sight, the next task would obviously be to decide whether determinism is actually true, or whether it can be given up, in favour of what we all naturally incline to believe. But before this task can even be discussed, one other attempt at reconciling the opposing views must be noticed. It is sometimes suggested that although determinism, that is belief in the possibility of a complete causal explanation of all aspects of human behaviour, is not compatible with our ordinary language of choices, motives, and decisions this need not worry us, because it is simply another, different, way of describing the same set of facts. That is, it is claimed that there are different explanations possible of human actions, which run parallel with one another and are not meant to overlap, and which therefore cannot contradict each other in any worrying way. This sort of suggestion was put forward, for instance, by S. E. Toulmin and by A. N. Flew, in *Analysis*, 1948 and 1949.[1] The trouble, however, with this solution is that it is so simple that it fails even to look for very long like a solution. In a recent discussion of the problem Austin Farrer puts this proposed solution into the mouth of an imaginary philosopher, and then goes on to suggest that it does not work.[2] The philosopher says,

Do not we keep describing different aspects of things under different linguistic conventions? Isn't that how language works? And what is there to worry us if we find ourselves talking both personal life language and neurophysical language about the human body? The physical language is to tell us how it works and what it will do; the personal life language expresses how it feels itself from inside.

To which the objection is made as follows:

What could sound more unexceptionable? That is how language works: it expresses different aspects of things under different conventions of speech; or, to put it more philosophically, we find that

[1] *Analysis*, December 1948, 'The Logical Status of Psycho-analysis', October 1949, 'Psycho-analytic Explanation'.

[2] *The Freedom of the Will*, chapter IV, pp. 63 *sqq*.

by using different conventions of speech we can arrive at descriptions which are useful in different ways. Certainly. But do we make it a linguistic rule, never to attempt the relating to one another of our different descriptions? . . . Did anyone ever doubt that these two lines of talk employed different types of description? But it remains to ask, how the matters they describe go together in one world. The general analogy of multiple descriptions will cast no light on so particular a question.

Farrer then proceeds to compare different analogous cases of multiple descriptions with the multiple description of human behaviour, to see whether these help to answer the question of inter-relation of the two ways of talking, and he finds that they do not. His conclusion, therefore, is that we are left with the question unanswered of which is the *proper* way to describe human behaviour, or whether one type of explanation is not fundamental and the other superficial. Although Farrer's argument from analogy does not conclusively prove that no account could be found which would relate the two ways of talking which he mentions, nor does it conclusively prove even that they need to be related, it does appear strongly to suggest that the proposal of his imagined linguistic philosopher is too weak to be of much use in what we are still inclined to feel is a real issue between determinism and common sense.

If, then, it is an issue, if neither of the proposed methods of reconciliation will work, it would be highly desirable to find out once and for all whether determinism was true or false. The chief obstacle in the way of doing this has so far been that no determinist can be found to state clearly exactly what determinism commits him to. To speak vaguely of causal explanation of human behaviour is not enough; for although any determinist would presumably hold that causal explanation of some kind was possible, there might be great differences between determinists on such matters as whether the explanation of human conduct was to be mechanical or in terms of regularity of response to stimulus, for example; and about whether the explanation had to be practically, or only theoretically, possible. All these points, and many more, would need to be clarified before a satisfactory argument could even begin. It seems that the doctrines called determinism have usually been stated by

persons who either do not wish to accept them, or who wish to
show that they are in no way incompatible with our ordinary
beliefs about human behaviour. Such persons would not form
the best advocates for the view, and it is quite likely that they
have constructed a kind of bogus doctrine containing elements
from many different sources, which would not stand up to
critical examination for long. The difficulty is that so far no
one has tried very hard to state the case coherently. But the
usual form in which the issue is presented is as turning upon
the possibility of the predictability of human choices. If it is
true that there could be a genuine causal account of any human
choice, then it follows that any human choice should be predictable, by reference to these same causal laws. Now it is clear
at once, and has frequently been pointed out, that not all kinds
of predictability are incompatible with freedom of choice. If,
for instance, I predict that someone whose character I respect
and whom I know to be consistent will refuse a bribe, and if I
turn out to be right, this does not, even for a moment, suggest
that he did not freely choose to refuse the bribe. But the possibility of prediction of this kind is wholly irrelevant to the issue,
since although it is doubtless based on inductive evidence, it is
not in any sense a causal prediction; it is not the kind of prediction which would be backed up by an explanation of any
kind at all, or at least it need not be. It is very different from a
prediction that if I give a child soneryl he will go to sleep. This
is a prediction which is genuinely based on a causal law, and if
I am asked why he will go to sleep I need not just say 'because
he is that sort of child'; I can say something about the general
effects on people of the ingredients of soneryl. It is prediction
of this second, fully causal, kind which would be fatal to human
choice. If it is possible for me to say 'Always in this kind of
circumstance a person of this kind must choose such and such',
and if I really mean that he must, and that his choice is the
effect of the circumstances, then the feeling which the agent
may have that there is something open, that it is up to him to
decide what to do, must be an illusion. But it is not yet certain
that prediction of this kind is ever possible, still less that it
could ever be widely practised. The onus is upon the determinist, if only one could be found, to show that it does, or even

N.B.

"must choose" — how odd; yet it seems quite right
and indicates that the whole problem is being
misconceived for failure to understand the
human person.

that it might occur. This may seem like an evasion of the issue, but it is very hard to face an issue squarely when one does not know exactly what is supposed to be conflicting with what.

There is one further point which is perhaps worth mentioning before I leave the topic of free will: it is not clear that there could ever be a time when the idea of free choice was useless, whatever further discoveries in psychology or neurology were made. For although it might be possible to regard other people as wholly causally determined it would be very difficult if not impossible to regard oneself in the same light. This is a very obvious point which has often been made before, but it is not perhaps wholly irrelevant. It is very often difficult to avoid making a decision, and in some cases passivity is as much a decision as any other. Now even if someone else could tell you in advance the causes which would make you decide one way rather than another, it is unlikely that you would at the time of decision know all the relevant factors in the situation. For some of the things which the other person would have to know in order to predict your choice would be what features in the situation would appeal to you as reasons. You could not discover this for yourself without weighing them up *as* reasons. As soon as you started to do this, instead of trying to predict your own choice you would actually be choosing. For an important part of choice is deciding what is a reason worth taking into account and what is not. Thus it seems unlikely that the concepts of decision and choice could conceivably be eliminated, whatever the theoretical possibilities of prediction might be. But it *is* conceivable that the language which we use of our own choices and that which we use of other people's might come to be rather different, and I am not sure that there is not already a considerable difference between them.

The problem of free will, then, has been a good deal discussed in the last few years, but not solved. Some of the discussion, especially that which stemmed from Moore's chapter in *Ethics*, has turned out, in my opinion, to have been misconceived and not to have advanced the subject very far. But this does not mean that it was not worth trying. And in the course of the discussion of free will a number of other interesting subjects have been brought to light, among them the nature *most!*

of such concepts as 'act', 'choice', 'will', 'intention', and others of this general kind. I want now to say a little about the exploratory and analytical work which has been done on these topics.

Like some of the other topics discussed in this book, the group of subjects with which we are now concerned has little specifically to do with ethics. The borderline between moral philosophy and the rest of philosophy becomes at this point impossible to draw. But there is a group of related problems, roughly speaking the philosophy of mind, some of which have particular bearing upon human actions and choices. These may reasonably be considered as a part of moral philosophy, even though they tell us nothing about ethics, or about the difference between right and wrong. It has increasingly come to be felt, indeed, that without an adequate conceptual map of these psychological areas, ethics in the narrow sense is impossible, or at least, futile. This feeling has arisen largely as a result of the influence of Ludwig Wittgenstein. As far as concerns moral philosophy, by far the most important change that he brought about was a new interest in description of phenomena, rather than the framing of abstract theories of human behaviour. Wherever a philosophical problem has arisen, as for instance around the concept of 'the Will', in Wittgenstein's view what is needed is a thorough investigation of the language in which the problem has arisen, and still more of the language in the context of which the problematic word is used in real life. Only in this way can the concept be clarified, and the false pictures by which philosophers have been deceived be done away with. It is necessary to find out what the various words we use are used *for*. He says:

We must do away with all *explanation*, and description alone must take its place. And this description gets its power of illumination, i.e. its purpose, from the philosophical problems. These are, of course, not empirical problems, they are solved, rather, by looking into the workings of our language, and that in such a way as to make us recognize those workings: in despite of an urge to misunderstand them. The problems are solved not by giving new information, but by arranging what we have always known. Philosophy is a battle against the bewitchment of our intelligence by means of language.[1]

[1] L. Wittgenstein, *Philosophical Investigations*, p. 47, paragraph 109.

Let us look at some of the descriptions which Wittgenstein himself embarked upon. In the passage I shall quote, by way of example, he is discussing the concept of the Will. He is examining the view that willing is an experience, something which just happens and cannot be brought about.[1]

[613] In the sense in which I can ever bring anything about (such as stomach-ache through over-eating), I can also bring about an act of willing. In this sense I bring about the act of willing to swim by jumping into the water. Doubtless I was trying to say: I can't will willing; that is it makes no sense to speak of willing willing. 'Willing' is not the name of an action; and so not the name of a voluntary action either. And my use of a wrong expression came from our wanting to think of willing as an immediate non-causal bringing about. A misleading analogy lies at the root of this idea; the causal nexus seems to be established by a mechanism connecting two parts of a machine. The connexion may be broken if the mechanism is disturbed. [614] When I raise my arm 'voluntarily' I do not use any instrument to bring the movement about. My wish is not such an instrument either. [615] Willing, if it is not to be a sort of wishing, must be the action itself. It cannot be allowed to stop anywhere short of the action. If it is the action, then it is so in the ordinary sense of the word; so it is speaking, writing, walking, lifting a thing, imagining something. But it is also trying, attempting, making an effort . . . to speak, to write, to lift a thing, to imagine something etc. One imagines the willing subject here as something without any mass (without any inertia); as a motor which has no inertia in itself to overcome. And so is only a mover not a moved. That is, one can say 'I will, but my body does not obey me' but not 'My will does not obey me' (Augustine). But in the sense in which I cannot fail to will, I cannot try to will either.

The discussion moves on, then, to touch upon doing, trying, voluntary action, intention, and meaning. No conclusions are asserted on any of these topics; it is not even always clear when Wittgenstein speaks in his own person and when in the person of someone who has succumbed to the temptations offered by language. But in every case the aim is to make clear, first what we think about the subject, and then how we talk about it, and so finally what is actually true about it. The description is thus always primarily a description of the way to talk about the subject; for only by showing how language is really used can the

[1] *op. cit.* p. 159, paragraphs 613 *sqq.*

conceptual confusions which it has generated be cleared up. But describing how to talk about a complicated subject is not very different from describing the complexities of the subject itself. The two cannot properly be distinguished. Our eyes are necessarily directed towards the facts.

The longest and most systematic treatment of this same group of problems is to be found in Ryle's book, *The Concept of Mind*, the central chapters of which have exercised a great influence upon all subsequent discussions. Here, although the intention and purpose of the book are virtually identical with Wittgenstein's, the tone is utterly different, and there is no shortage of conclusions. By way of example I shall quote one short paragraph, once again on the subject of the Will.[1]

Men are not machines, not even ghost-ridden machines. They are men . . . a tautology which is sometimes worth remembering. People often pose such questions as 'How does my mind get my hand to make the required movements?' and even 'What makes my hand do what my mind tells it to do?' Questions of these patterns are properly asked of certain chain-processes. The question 'What makes the bullet fly out of the barrel?' is properly answered by 'The expansion of gases in the cartridge'; the question 'What makes the cartridge explode?' is answered by reference to the percussion of the detonator; and the question 'How does my squeezing the trigger make the pin strike the detonator?' is answered by describing the mechanism of springs, levers and catches between the trigger and the pin. So when it is asked 'How does my mind get my finger to squeeze the trigger?' the form of the question presupposes that a further chain-process is involved, embodying still further tensions, releases and discharges, though this time mental ones. But whatever is the act or operation adduced as the first step of this postulated chain-process, the performance of it has to be described in just the same way as in ordinary life we describe the squeezing of the trigger by the marksman. Namely we say simply 'he did it' and not 'he did or underwent something else which caused it'.

Perhaps even this single quotation may serve to show both the differences between *The Concept of Mind* and the *Philosophical Investigations*, and their similarity of aim. Professor Ryle shows language at work, in a truly everyday context. The chapters which follow that from which this passage was taken, on

[1] Gilbert Ryle, *The Concept of Mind* (1949), chapter 3, pp. 81 *sqq.*

Emotions, Dispositions, and Self-knowledge all demonstrate the same refusal to admit nonsensical questions or mysterious answers. Until a word has been shown to be *able* to work in a straightforward and intelligible way, it is not allowed as a proper part of language. So, to return to the particular case of the will, the concept of action in general is clarified by the rejecting of certain bogus concepts which have accumulated round it, such as that of the will as a kind of cause. This is exactly what Wittgenstein too rejected, but less harshly. From the *Investigations* we get the feeling that there was a real reason why people may have come to think of the will as a cause. From *The Concept of Mind* we would infer that only an idiot could ever have thought so. It is the same with the other related subjects discussed in the succeeding chapters: we are induced to think what we really mean by such things as 'feeling', 'motive', 'pleasure', by seeing how these words come into our ordinary discourse. And any philosophical beliefs we may find ourselves half inclined to hold about them are ruled out if they fail to pass the practical test. A concept must have work to do before it is admissible. It may sometimes be felt that Ryle is a little ruthless. A great deal is thrown out, perhaps because he allows us to make use of only rather simple ideas, and therefore only simple language, in our everyday conversations. But all the same, there is a great deal of penetrating observation and accurate description, not so much of actions and feelings themselves as of how we talk about actions and feelings. Such problems as these have come to be generally regarded as forming a necessary part of the subject matter of ethics. For instance, Stuart Hampshire's book *Thought and Action* suggested that one could begin to talk of people's moral views, their beliefs about how they ought to behave, only against a background of understanding the problems involved in discussing how they do behave, what is meant by saying that they act intentionally, or that they *try* or *choose* to act in a particular way. Wittgenstein's influence has been most felt in this descriptive part of the subject matter of moral philosophy; but, as I hope to show in the next chapter, from a very different standpoint, the Existentialist philosophers were at the same time attempting an equally realistic and descriptive kind of ethics.

7

Existentialism: J.-P. Sartre

So far I have been concerned almost exclusively with moral philosophy which, whether written in England or in America, has been essentially written in the tradition of English empiricism. Since 1900, both here and in the United States, metaphysics has been virtually dead. The influence of Wittgenstein, as I hope I have suggested, opened the way for a much wider view of moral philosophy than was generally held at the beginning of the century; and this width of vision may lead to greater descriptive or even classificatory enterprises on the part of philosophers. But it can hardly lead back to metaphysics. Philosophers are more interested in saying what is true than in constructing large-scale super-scientific explanations of things. Moral philosophy shows no signs of being once again swallowed up into a huge philosophical system, built to explain the universe. But on the continent a very different sort of moral philosophy has been flourishing in the first half of this century, and I must now try to say something about this.

System-building has not been discredited on the continent and metaphysics has been practised in the Hegelian manner. Moral philosophy has taken a place as part of the general theory of man, of human nature and its place in the universe. The metaphysical style, too, has been perpetuated in continental philosophy, and we meet here once again the high tone, the obscurity, the wealth of technical terms, which have been so noticeably absent from English philosophy of the same period. Sometimes, it must be admitted, a kind of despair afflicts one when reading these philosophers. Surely, one feels like saying, we have outgrown all this. We have been through it all and, with the help of Moore and Ayer, we have struggled out the other side. But it would be a mistake to refuse, on either aesthetic or doctrinaire grounds, to make an effort to understand these philosophers. There is a great deal to be found, not only of that peculiar aesthetic satisfaction which, whether we believe in them or not, metaphysical theories of ethics are capable of providing, but also of illumination. For there is, especially in the works of Sartre, much acute criticism of other philosophers, and, most important, there are elaborate serious and imaginative descriptions of moral phenomena. It is at this point that the two different kinds of philosophy meet. With a different purpose, and under the influence of Wittgenstein, English moral philosophers are just beginning to explore this same territory. What we have referred to as the psychology of action and choice, which is coming to be the most interesting part of English moral philosophy, is of the greatest importance in existentialist philosophy. The phenomena thought to be relevant are not always the same, but the descriptive element is common.

It is obvious that in one chapter it would be impossible to give even a sketch of the whole field, and in any case I am not competent to do such a thing. To lump all continental moral philosophers together as existentialists is in itself an absurdity. But existentialism is broadly speaking what I want to discuss, and I shall therefore boldly select for discussion the one philosopher who has actually described himself as an existentialist, namely Sartre. It is hardly necessary to add that any reasonably complete study would include discussion of at least Kierkegaard, Heidegger, Jaspers, and Marcel as well. But these I shall not mention. Sartre has not only attached to himself this familiar label, but he is also the best known of these philosophers, and there is therefore some justification for discussing him alone. But it must not be forgotten that, in spite of family resemblances between his work and that of other continental philosophers, he does not speak for a group or school, but only for himself.

The term 'existentialist' is not self-explanatory. Sartre accounts for it in a popular lecture called 'Existentialism is a

Humanism', which he delivered in 1946.[1] This lecture is clear, but necessarily over-simplified. By itself it would do little to suggest the depth or complexity of Sartre's thought. It does, however, bring out unambiguously, and indeed with exaggeration, the basic concepts upon which the whole system rests. An existentialist, Sartre says, is one who holds that existence precedes essence. This mysterious belief is meant to have application only to the case of human beings; it is the distinctive feature of human beings, in fact, that their existence does precede their essence. Sartre contrasts a human being with an artifact, a paper-knife, which is first conceived by its maker, and then made. The idea of the paper-knife is that it should be of a certain kind and fulfil a certain function. It is of the essence of a paper-knife to be like this. Once it is conceived, its actual characteristics, when it comes into existence in the workshop, are already determined. This is what is meant by saying that its essence precedes its existence. Human beings, on the other hand, are not first conceived, and then made to a specification, or to fulfil a certain purpose. They exist, and what they are or what they become depends upon what they *do*. For this they are themselves wholly responsible. A man is not, for instance, a born cook, who then fulfils his function by cooking. On the contrary, he *chooses* to be a cook; he elects to fill up the blank space of his life in one way rather than another. His being a cook is not determined by anything, nor is it even justifiable by an appeal to his nature. He is, and has always been, perfectly free to do whatever he likes.

It is, above all, this attitude to human freedom and to human choice that the term 'existentialism' serves to mark off. There is of course very much more to it than this. But already it seems to me that two important points stand out. First, it is no doubt valuable to resist the Greek view that men have a certain function for which they were designed, and that the best anyone can do is to find out what this function is and to fulfil it. But by using the words 'essence' and 'existence' to bring out the difference between the Greek view and his own, Sartre seems to

[1] *L'existentialisme est un humanisme*. Published in England (Methuen, 1948) as *Existentialism and Humanism*, in U.S.A. as *Existentialism*, in Germany as *Ist der Existenzialismus ein Humanismus?*

be suggesting not only that people do not have functions, as paper-knives do, but that there is nothing *common to* human beings, or *essential to human nature*, which may limit their freedom of choice. He has to allow that there are common physical characteristics of man, and that physically men are limited by what is 'humanly possible'. But it seems absurd to suggest that there are no common psychological factors which may limit our choice just as much. The example of the paper-knife is in fact unfair. We may well want to agree that it is improper to describe human beings in the sort of terms appropriate for artifacts. But the contrast between essence and existence would be rather different, and rather more difficult to draw, if one took an animal instead of a paper-knife as an example. A horse may not have been designed to do some one job, but still we should want to say that, being a horse, it was determined to behave in certain broadly predictable ways. There is a whole number of things one could say were essential to horses, which limit the ways they can behave; the question of design or purpose need not come into it at all. It seems to me that there are common characteristics of men, too, and of types of men, in terms of which their behaviour is at least partially predictable, which the simple contrast with the paper-knife would not suggest. That Sartre himself was not really able to keep up the belief in pure existence is shown I think by his novels (or at least he could not keep up his interest in it). If the existentialist contention were true, people should be represented as perfectly individualistic, their characters entirely made up of actions which they have chosen themselves. But in fact one may well feel that a defect of Sartre as a novelist is that his characters have no individuality at all. They make decisions, certainly, but they make them as people of a certain type. We tend to forget their names and remember them as 'a traitor', 'a Fascist', 'a homosexual'. It is as if in the last resort Sartre were interested in essences after all, at least in the sense of characteristics in virtue of which people may be regarded as typical of a class. Individual personality, which, according to the theory, should be created every moment by free choices, seems to have been squeezed out, and an abstract freedom of choice has taken its place, which demands that the agent be regarded as an abstract entity as well.

The second difficulty in this concept of free choice is perhaps more serious. It seems to me simply false that we choose everything that we do and that we are, from our childhood on. To say that we choose every aspect of our characters, that we are nothing at all except what we *choose* to be, has a certain rhetorical and salutary effect; but, at the very least, it distorts the meaning of the word 'choose'. It is true that we are probably responsible for more of our attitudes and emotions as well as for more of our actions than we are sometimes inclined to think; and it is good for us to be reminded that expressions like 'I could not help feeling . . .' may well be false, or a prelude to mere excuses. Perhaps we are *responsible* for all the attitudes which we find that we have accepted over the years. But to say that we *choose* to adopt them is not true. Choice and responsibility should be distinguished. We need to keep the word 'choice' for some more definite and datable occurrence. We should know when we are choosing, at the very least. But perhaps this objection is not so very serious after all. To say that each one of us has absolute freedom, and to say that he is only what he chooses to be and nothing else—both of these are exaggerations, but they succeed in defining an outlook which is intelligible and from which (more or less), as I hope I shall show, moral philosophy can be fruitfully pursued. In order to show this, it is necessary to go rather more deeply into the metaphysical theory of which Sartre's moral philosophy forms a part.

Sartre's most important philosophical work is *L'Être et le Néant*, of which an English translation was published in 1956.[1] A great deal of the book consists not of arguments but of examples and of long descriptions of psychological phenomena. Moreover, it is written in an extraordinarily thick, obscure style, full of technical terms of a grotesque kind, derived from Hegel. As one reads through the book one comes to accept these terms as perfectly natural and indeed the only terms in which the thought could have been expressed. The danger is that in discussing it one may either reproduce nothing at all except the darkness and obscurity of the original, or, if one tries to expound the thought in plain language, one may be left with

[1] *L'Être et le Néant*. Paris: Gallimard, 1943. Translated into English by Hazel E. Barnes as *Being and Nothingness*.

something unduly thin and platitudinous, from which all the interest has been removed with the obscurity. In the light of these difficulties I shall attempt not a summary nor a full exposition of Sartre's doctrines but something like an impression of them. It should not be forgotten that to someone else they might appear in a different light.

Sartre, like all French philosophers, starts from Descartes. His aim, like Descartes', is to see how much can be derived from a consideration of consciousness, or thinking in the very widest sense. Like Descartes, he wants to pick on an instantaneous moment of consciousness and derive his conclusions from this. But while Descartes could prove (at least directly) only the existence of himself as a thinking being, Sartre claims to go further. This departure from the master is of the greatest consequence; it marks, in fact, a total rejection of the Cartesian philosophy. He holds that the very essence of consciousness is that it should be directed towards some object. The powerful influence of the phenomenologists, particularly of Husserl, is thus apparent right at the beginning: it is taken as something which hardly needs explanation that consciousness is 'intensional'; that even apparently 'pure' states of mind or feeling have some external object. If a man says to himself, therefore, in a Cartesian spirit, 'I think,' he can deduce from this the existence not only of himself but of objects of thought, things in the world and other people, so that merely to be conscious is already to enter into some sort of relation with the world. This is a point of fundamental importance. In trying to state what this relation is, we come upon the first serious difficulty in Sartre's terminology. What distinguishes a conscious being from an unconscious being is that in consciousness there is a gap between the consciousness and that which is its object. This gap is referred to as 'nothingness'; but there is an obvious defect in this, apart from its manifest unintelligibility. To use the noun 'nothingness' is almost bound in the end to lead to the suggestion that nothingness is a *thing*, though of a peculiar kind. If, furthermore, the presence of this characteristic nothingness is actually the distinguishing mark of the conscious being, then the temptation to think of it as a thing of some positive kind is almost overwhelming. It is better therefore, as far as I can see, to avoid the word altogether, even though it occurs in the very title of the book, and to speak instead of 'a gap' or 'an emptiness' within the conscious being, which he is always trying to fill by thinking and by acting. But besides this meaning—that of the emptiness or blank within the conscious being—there is another meaning of 'nothingness' which in turn serves to mark off the conscious being from the unconscious. Conscious beings are able to form negative judgements, and thus to distinguish both themselves from other things, and other things one from another. A man who thinks, that is, is able to realize that a house is not a tree, and that he himself is not a tree; and he may go further. Through this possibility of forming negative judgements, he may realize that today he is not what he will be to-morrow and so to understand that what he will be tomorrow is not anything at all, yet. So the possibility of framing such judgements is essential to a man's realization of his own freedom to be this or to be that in the future.

The conscious being is referred to by Sartre, borrowing from Hegel, as the *being-for-itself*. Unconscious beings are *beings-in-themselves*. They are thought of as thoroughly existing in a solid concrete way. The whole of their possibilities are, as it were, absorbed in being a chair or a tree. Whatever thoughts or attitudes we may have concerning them, beings-in-them-selves go on existing undisturbed, and completely determined by their own nature to be as they are. They are more than just our perception of them. Consciousness is regarded as the very opposite of this. Beings-for-themselves bring nothingness into the world, both in the sense of emptiness—a failure to be *any-thing*, and in the sense of negation—a being-for-itself knows that it does *not* have this pure concrete solid existence which trees and chairs have, and it strives above all things to have such existence, unsuccessfully. Consciousness, therefore, con-sisting as it does of this emptiness waiting to be filled up, and of this knowledge that it is *not* any of the solid and permanent beings-in-themselves, must, if it exists at all, exist in relation to external objects, whose existence in the world does not need further proof. From this starting-point Sartre sets out to ex-plore more completely the relations which do in fact hold between conscious beings and the rest of the world.

E

It is noticeable that even into what purports to be a bare statement of Sartre's most general views, words like 'strive' and 'unsuccessful' inevitably creep in. This is not chance. In exploring further the relations which he supposes to hold between conscious beings and the outside world, we shall need to employ a whole battery of such words. Conscious beings, beings-for-themselves, *desire* being-in-itself; they feel *nausea* at the contemplation of the multiplicity and disorderliness of things in the world; they feel *anguish* at the realization of their own freedom. Now it may well be objected that the words 'nausea' and 'anguish' are emotive to a very high degree, that Sartre could have made the very same philosophical points in different terms. When he wished to express the thought, fundamental to his system, that human life is not determined, and that it cannot be justified by any appeal to something outside itself, he says that human life is 'absurd'. Once again it may be objected that he could make a perfectly good point against any theorists who want to explain or justify human life, by simply denying what they say, and without using the powerfully emotive word 'absurd'. It is necessary to notice this objection straight away since the offending words play so important a part in the whole structure of existentialist thought. There is, I think, a perfectly good reason why words of this type come into the exposition of Sartre's views. His metaphysical system is concerned with human nature not as the uniquely cognitive element in the world, but as the uniquely active, non-determined element. The contrast he is constantly insisting upon is not that between the knower and what he knows, between mind-substance and body-substance (which is the typically Cartesian dualism); he is concerned with the contrast between the natural world, governed by rigidly deterministic laws, and dynamic human nature, which has its own power of action within it, and which is free to make itself what it chooses. Sartre is of course not the first to concern himself with this dualism instead of the other. It has indeed quite properly been characterized as Kantian. But it follows that any description of the human situation in relation to the external world will inevitably be in terms of doing things, of choices, projects, and attitudes. Emotions are regarded as partial and frustrated actions; therefore what a man *feels* on contemplating the world is as relevant to his situation as what he actually does. Any account of human nature must above all, on this view, concern itself with human motives. Thus the concepts of desiring, striving, trying—all these must necessarily be employed. But what about nausea and anguish? and what about absurdity? Here once again what there is, I think, is exaggeration. It is not that such concepts are irrelevant altogether to philosophy; it is that the actual words used go too far. They may mislead, if people pick just on them without seeing how they fit into the whole metaphysical picture of man. But just as it is not accidental that Sartre should exaggerate in his insistence upon human responsibility and freedom of choice, so his use of words like 'absurd' to describe the human situation is not accidental. He means to produce a certain impression, as well as to expound a system. Nor is he the first metaphysician to have such an intention.

To return now to the exposition: when confronted by the awareness of the variety, contingency, and senselessness of the world, a conscious being feels nausea. He longs to be able to class things neatly into kinds, and to see some sort of necessity of their being in this kind or in that. When he thinks of his own life, he wants to be able to regard that in the same way as something which is orderly and which has a certain pattern. But he finds that he cannot. Even language turns out to be misleading, simply because it does suggest that things can be pinned down by having their appropriate name attached to them. But in fact the existence of things escapes from this artificial restraint imposed by words. Of peculiar importance in explaining this nausea which we are supposed to feel, is the concept of the viscous. In part four, chapter two, of *Being and Nothingness*, in a section called 'Quality as a revelation of being', Sartre says that what we need is a psycho-analysis of things. He then considers the case of viscous sticky things, half liquid half solid, and he finds that this viscosity is a fundamental category of material things, which has a peculiar fascination for us, as well as filling us with disgust. That our attitude to it should be of this kind is wholly natural; we do not have to be taught to regard it in this way; as soon as we are aware of objects at all we are aware of this aspect of them. The secret of our attitude is that the viscous is naturally ambiguous. It is neither solid nor liquid. We may think we can touch it, or pick it up like solid stuff, but it eludes us. It is not, on the other hand, like water which we know we cannot pick up and possess. If something is viscous and sticky we may think we can pick it up 'only, at the very moment when I believe that I possess it, by a curious reversal, it possesses me'. It is impossible to get rid of. It clings to our hands. Now it is clear how we may use the viscous as a symbol of things in the external world, and Sartre says that we do so use it. His point is also that we are not *taught* to regard it as symbolic. It comes to us already symbolizing other objects and ourselves, which we constantly feel we should be able to grasp and possess, only to find that we cannot. Just when we may think that we have it, we are sucked back into the sticky, senseless mass of objects and of our own random and pointless acts in the past. To escape from the viscosity of things would be to be able to see one's own life as an ordered inevitable pattern, and to see oneself as a solid being-in-itself, moving inevitably among other hard, solid, predictable objects. The viscous, then, is a ready-made symbol of the situation in which we find ourselves. That is why we feel a sickly horror when we contemplate it.

Connected with the nausea which we feel when we realize our situation with regard to the objects around us is the anguish which we experience when we turn our attention to ourselves. Nausea is brought on by our inability to organize and separate objects, and our tendency to be overwhelmed by them and sucked into the general mess. Anguish is brought on by the reflection that there is nothing at all to determine our choices. Our past is separated from us by the perpetual gap which arises in our consciousness. We may suppose that by acting in this way or in that, we have determined ourselves to a certain course in the future. But, if we are still conscious at all, as soon as our acts become past acts, the emptiness within us reasserts itself. We are forced to *think* about our past, not just to have it drive us forward. And just as there thus arises a gap between the past and the present, which prevents our ever saying we were *caused* to do this or that by what had happened before, so there is equally a gap between us and the future, which may be filled in anyhow we choose. But whatever we choose, we can never hope finally to justify it, nor can we be sure that any value attaches to it at all. Thus we feel anguish before the recognition that we have to choose, but that the choice is for nothing.

But of course Sartre is perfectly prepared to allow that we do not feel either nausea or anguish all, or even much, of the time. How then do we avoid them? Sartre's answer to this is absolutely fundamental to what may be called his moral philosophy and his psychology. The answer is that we avoid them by means of *mauvaise foi*—bad faith. The whole of the first part of *L'Être et le Néant* is indeed centred round the question, 'How must we describe the human consciousness if it is to be capable of bad faith?' Let us examine, as far as we can, what Sartre understands by bad faith. Essentially it is a denial of our freedom of choice. If we see ourselves as bound to act in a certain way, if we feel inclined to say, 'I have no choice in the matter,' then we are deceiving ourselves. Bad faith is a kind of self-deception. It involves playing a role, and regarding our behaviour as determined by the role we play. It is the failure to realize that even what role to play has originally been a matter of choice and that it remains a matter of choice whether to continue in the role or not. Bad faith operates at various levels. It covers the superficial self-deception with the help of which, for instance, we might justify some extravagance by saying, 'I really need it,' or 'This is a good time to buy; next year they will be even more expensive.' It also covers more basic self-deceptions by means of which one might, for instance, excuse one's political inertia by claiming that it was just not part of one's character to interest oneself in such things, or that one had been brought up not to do so. The moment one is introduced to the concept of bad faith, it can be seen to have infinite explanatory possibilities. There are many people, for instance, about whom one would hesitate to say that they were insincere, or that they knowingly or fully deliberately pretended to be what they were not. But nevertheless one feels about these people that they are always seeing themselves as such and such —a member of some social group, an intellectual, a mother; and that all their tastes and views are, for the time being, dictated by the part they see themselves in. For this kind of person the concept of bad faith is useful. It is worth considering some of the examples which Sartre himself gives in *Being and Nothingness*.

Take the example [he says][1] of a woman who has consented to go out with a particular man for the first time. She knows very well the intentions which the man who is speaking to her cherishes regarding her, she knows also that it will be necessary sooner or later for her to make a decision. But she does not want to realize the urgency. She does not apprehend this conduct as an attempt to achieve what we call 'the first approach': that is, she does not want to see possibilities of temporal development which his conduct presents. She restricts this behaviour to what is present; she does not wish to read into the phrases which he addresses to her anything except their explicit meaning. If he says to her, 'I find you so attractive', she disarms this phrase of its sexual background; she attaches to the conversation and to the behaviour of the speaker the immediate meanings, which she imagines as objective qualities. The man who is speaking to her appears to her sincere and respectful, just as the table is round or square, as the wall colouring is grey or blue. The qualities thus attached to the person she is listening to are in this way fixed in a permanence like that of things. . . . But then suppose he takes her hand. This act of her companion risks changing the situation by calling for an immediate decision. To leave the hand there is to consent in herself to flirt, to engage herself. To withdraw it is to break the troubled and unstable harmony which gives the hour its charm. The aim is to postpone the moment of decision as long as possible. We know what happens next: the young woman leaves her hand there, but she *does not notice* that she is leaving it. She does not notice it because it happens by chance that she is at this moment all intellect. She draws her companion up to the most lofty regions of sentimental speculation; she speaks of life, of her life, she shows herself in her essential aspect—a personality, a consciousness. And during this time the divorce of the body from the soul is accomplished; the hand rests inert between the warm hands of her companion—neither consenting nor resisting . . . a thing.

I shall quote extensively from one further example, from the same part of the book, which seems to me particularly illuminating.

---

[1] *op. cit.* part 2, chapter 2.

Let us consider [Sartre says] the waiter in the café. His movement is quick and forward, a little too precise, a little too rapid. He comes towards the patrons with a step a little too quick. He bends forward a little too eagerly; his voice, his eyes express an interest a little too solicitous for the order of the customer. Finally he returns, trying to imitate in his walk the inflexible stiffness of some kind of automaton while carrying his tray with the recklessness of a tight-rope walker by putting it in a perpetually unstable, perpetually broken equilibrium which he perpetually re-establishes by a light movement of the arm and hand. All his behaviour seems to us a game, but what is he playing? We need not watch long before we can explain it: he is playing *at being* a waiter in a café. There is nothing there to surprise us. The game is a kind of marking out and investigating. The child plays with his own body in order to explore it, to take inventory of it; the waiter in the café plays with his condition in order to *realize it*. This obligation is not different from that which is imposed on all tradesmen. Their condition is wholly one of ceremony. The public demands of them that they realize it as a ceremony; there is the dance of the grocer, of the tailor, of the auctioneer, by which they endeavour to persuade their clientele that they are nothing but a grocer, an auctioneer, a tailor. A grocer who dreams is offensive to the buyer, because such a grocer is not wholly a grocer. Society demands that he limit himself to his function as a grocer, just as a soldier on duty makes himself into a soldier-thing with a direct regard which does not see at all, which is no longer meant to see, since it is the rule and not the interest of the moment which determines the point he must fix his eyes on. . . . There are indeed many precautions to imprison a man in what he is, as if we lived in perpetual fear that he might escape from it, that he might break away and suddenly elude his condition. . . . From within, the waiter in the café cannot immediately be a café waiter in the sense that this inkwell is an inkwell or the glass is a glass. It is by no means that he cannot form reflective judgements or concepts concerning his condition. He knows well what it 'means': the obligation of getting up at five o'clock, of sweeping the floor of the shop before the restaurant opens, of starting the coffee pot going, etc. He knows the rights which it allows: the right to the tips, the right to belong to a union, etc. But all these concepts, all these judgements refer to the transcendent. It is a matter of abstract possibilities, of rights and duties conferred on a 'person possessing rights'. And it is precisely this person *who I have to be* (if I am the waiter in question) and who I am not. . . . If I represent myself as him, I am not he: I am separated from him as the object from the subject, separated by *nothing*, but this nothing isolates me from him. I cannot be he, I can only play at *being* him, that is imagine to myself that I am he. What I attempt to realize is a being-in-itself of the café waiter, as if it were not in my power to confer their value and their urgency upon my duties and the rights of my position, as if it were not my free choice to get up at five o'clock each morning or to remain in bed, even though it meant getting fired. As if from the very fact that I sustain this role in existence I did not transcend it on every side, as if I did not constitute myself as one beyond my condition. Yet there is no doubt that I *am* in a sense a café waiter . . . otherwise could I not just as well call myself a diplomat or a reporter? But if I am one, this cannot be in the mode of being-in-itself. I am a waiter in the mode of *Being-what-I-am-not*.

These examples, each in its different way, show that the person who exhibits bad faith does so in order to try to become an object, a being-in-itself, without consciousness and without, therefore, the necessity of choosing what to do. He wishes to be something with fixed describable properties in virtue of the possession of which he is *determined to* behave in this way or in that. In the first example, the woman not only wishes to regard herself in this light but she wishes to regard the man in the same way. She has attached to him the label 'sincerity' and therefore she simply does not choose to notice anything except what bears out this description of him. She treats herself equally as an object. There is her hand, lying there. She is not responsible for it. It is simply a thing occupying a certain spatial position, and meanwhile *she* is concerned with higher things. But of course she has *chosen* to dissociate herself in this way from her hand. She is trading on the undeniable fact that her hand is an object in the world. But it is not only this and cannot, with good faith, be treated as if it were. In the second example, the waiter is likewise attempting to be a waiter in the way in which an inkwell is an inkwell. That is to say, he is pretending that waiters are simply *compelled* to behave in the way he behaves, in virtue of the fact that they are waiters. But he is not, as the woman was, trying to pretend that he is an object in the world. He is trading rather on the fact that everybody is an object of attention to other people. He knows that in the eyes of others he is just a waiter, that indeed they want him to be just a waiter; and therefore he aims to live up to this view and be nothing except what they think him. By doing this he manages, more or less, to obscure from himself the truth, namely that at any moment he could stop behaving as he does; and that if he gets up at five each morning it is because he chooses to do so. This concept of being-for-others is of great importance, and I want to come back to it in a moment. First, however, there are one or two points which arise out of the concept of bad faith in general.

Bad faith is the protection which we assume against the torments of nausea and anguish. Any evasion of responsibility is an instance of bad faith; any denial that we can be other than we are. One of the kinds of bad faith which Sartre attacks is a reliance upon Freudian psycho-analysis as an explanation of human conduct. The subconscious mind he regards as magic— a pseudo-explanation invoked by persons who cannot or will not understand their true motives. Nearly all his descriptions of psychological phenomena and of human behaviour have the precise point of offering an alternative explanation, to supersede the Freudian. But there is in Sartre's explanations a defect which is at times shared by Freud's, namely that it is absolutely impossible to refute it, or even deny its applicability, since every refusal to accept it is taken as yet one more piece of evidence in its favour. For instance, suppose that one denied, as I think one very well might, that nausea was what one experienced when contemplating the external world. Suppose that, to be more specific still, one denied that the viscosity of things had any particular effect on one at all; suppose one said the suggestion that viscosity is an important category of the material was nothing but neurotic . . . would not all these denials be taken simply as instances of bad faith? They probably would. If bad faith can be crudely defined as the refusal to face disagreeable facts, then one's denials can always be construed as such a refusal. And the more vigorous one's protests that this is not self-deception, that it is only to falsehoods or exaggerations that one is objecting, the more serious the accusation of bad faith would become. Such obstinacy could be interpreted as a fault of character, not a desire for truth. At the very least, Sartre has neurotically over-emphasized what may be a tiny fact about some people's attitude to the world. And it cannot be denied that there is something insanely arbitrary and partial in picking out just *this* quality of things for so much attention. The difficulty with any philosophy whose method is largely descriptive is brought out by this case. It is impossible to describe *all* the objects or situations or qualities in the universe. So whatever is selected is likely to have the appearance of having been selected at random. There can be no justification, as far as I can see, for picking on one aspect of the world rather than another. The test cannot be completeness; it must be rather whether the description succeeds in conveying *some* kind of feeling, some attitude to the world. By this test, Sartre's descriptions certainly succeed. But it is going too far, in the light of this partial success, to hope to explain the whole of the universe and human conduct in the terms introduced into the description.

As I have suggested already there is one important aspect of existentialism which must still be discussed. This is the question of a man's relation not to objects in the external world, but to other men. We have seen that in two different ways a man of bad faith may try to become a *thing* and thus deny his responsibility for what he does. The first way is to try to become just a physical object: it is worth remarking here that Sartre, like Berkeley and other metaphysicians, has a powerful feeling for the texture of the universe. It does not seem to him extraordinary to search for some one word which would characterize all physical things—indeed the word he picks on is '*massif*' . . . solid. 'The in-itself has nothing secret.' 'It has no within which is opposed to a without.' In a sense we can designate it as a synthesis; but it is the most indissoluble of all: the synthesis of itself with itself. Human beings, then, are not '*massif*' in this way, and part of their perpetual quest is to become so— to have no opposition of the within to the without. Since no one wants to become *unconscious*, although he longs for solid being-in-itself, and since consciousness is what produces the lack of solidity in men, the quest is contradictory. But sometimes it may take the form of seeking to be God—for God could be described as the possessor of just these contradictory qualities— namely consciousness and being-in-itself. (It is therefore senseless, Sartre says, to ask whether God exists. 'God' is the name of something to be arrived at, which it is impossible to achieve.)

The second thing that a man of bad faith may attempt to do is to become nothing but an object for others. The fact that we are each of us an object for others is an essential component in our existence as human beings. It helps to define our situation as specifically human. For instance, suppose I had been on a desert island alone for so long that I had lost the concept of other people. Then I might come to think that the way I chose to do things was literally the only possible way. The fact that things could be looked at from another viewpoint would escape me, and therefore I might fail to realize that I myself occupied some particular viewpoint which I could change at will, and by thus being unaware of my freedom I would be less than human. In the third part of *Being and Nothingness*, Sartre sets out to explore the concept of the existence of others. In spite of its extreme length and repetitiveness, this seems to me one of the most interesting parts of the whole book. He starts with a criticism of solipsism, and an account of the views of Husserl, Heidegger, and Hegel. In the section entitled 'The look'[1] he finally states his own view of what the relation is between myself and other people. He argues that in our awareness of other people we do not first apprehend them as physical objects of a particular kind, and then argue, by analogy, that they have consciousness, that they can feel and think. It is rather that our first apprehension of them strikes us immediately as incomplete. We have the feeling that, unlike other material objects which we perceive, here is one which can escape us, and which necessarily partially eludes us. This is neither an inference from perception, nor a kind of mysterious or mystical awareness of someone else's mind. It is, Sartre says, like ordinary perception with a hole in it. He takes the example of seeing a man reading a book as he walks in the park.

There is a full object for me to grasp. In the midst of the universe I can say 'man reading' as I could say 'cold stone', 'fine rain'. I apprehend a closed 'gestalt' in which the reading forms an essential quality; for the rest, it remains blind and mute, lets itself be known as a pure

[1] *op. cit.* part 3, chapter 1, section IV.

and simple temporal-spatial thing. . . . The quality 'man reading' as the relation of the man to the book is simply a little particular crack in my universe. At the heart of this solid visible form, he makes himself a particular emptying. The form is solid only in appearance; its peculiar meaning is to be—in the midst of my universe, at ten paces from me, at the heart of that solidity—a closely consolidated localized flight.

But this is not the whole truth about the relation between myself and the Other. So far the Other still appears as a mere object, though of a peculiar kind. The key to the unique relation between me and the Other is that I am an object for him; he can look at me. I am not able to consider this exactly as I consider his looking at anything else—say grass. The difference is that being looked at by another person actually affects me. Sartre considers the case of soldiers who are trying to escape the notice of the enemy. In this case they do not think of the look of the enemy as necessarily connected with a particular man whose eyes they can see looking at them. They regard bushes and houses—all sorts of cover—as places from which the look may come.

What I apprehend immediately when I hear the branches crackling behind me is not that there is someone there; it is that I am vulnerable, that I have a body which can be hurt, that I occupy a place, and that I can not in any case escape from the space in which I am without defence—in short that I am seen.

He then goes on to raise the question 'What does being seen mean for me?' In the next example he considers the case of a man who out of curiosity, or jealousy, looks and listens at a keyhole. While he is engaged in this, his whole concentration is fixed upon what he is doing, and upon what he hears and sees. In a sense he is unaware of himself; in a sense his 'self' does not yet exist, because he is nothing except the act of looking and listening. But then, while he is in this attitude, he becomes aware that he has heard footsteps, and that someone has come up behind him. The realization that there is someone watching him alters his whole mode of existence. He becomes aware of himself in a way that he was not before. He suddenly feels ashamed. Shame, Sartre says, is a confession that it was he doing the act of which he is ashamed; later he will try to get round the memory of the incident by bad faith. But even bad faith is a confession. So self-awareness, guilt, shame, and pride all come into existence at the glance of the other, and it is in this sense that it is possible to say that the existence of the person, the for-itself, is actually dependent on the existence of another person. Without it, no one would be able to conceive any definition of himself. The discussion of shame and pride is curiously perfunctory, and it is impossible not to be reminded of Hume's discussions of the same subject, and to feel that his conclusions were not so very different and his manner of reaching them less exhausting. But all the same Sartre has, in the discussion of the Other in general, called attention to a number of extremely important points. First, he has noticed the inadequacy of any theory which suggests that other people are, for us, just material objects which we invest, imaginatively, with inner life on an analogy with our own. Of course analogy plays an enormous part in our understanding of individual human beings; but it is very hard to believe that our primary awareness of the existence of others can be explained in these terms. The fact that we are objects of perception, of attention for them, the fact that they are obstacles for us, and make plans in which we have no share, but which affect our plans—these things seem to me, as Sartre suggests, far more basic to our realization both of other people and of our own consequent situation in the world. Secondly, Sartre draws our attention to the difficulties inherent in the difference between our own view of ourselves and other people's view of us. These are partly difficulties of language; from our own point of view it is usually very difficult to accept any description of ourselves. Even though I might admit that, for instance, I worked in a bank, I should repudiate the suggestion that I was a bank clerk. Though I might admit that I sometimes took things which did not belong to me, I should resist the designation 'thief'. But for other people, who see me from the outside, there is no other appropriate description except 'bank clerk' or 'thief'. And reflecting on these words, I may come to feel that since I would not use them, while someone else would, of the very same object, therefore their meaning is somehow destroyed. Again, there is a familiar difficulty about the predictability of a man's behaviour. He is filled with horror when he first realizes that people regard him as in certain ways predictable. He suddenly sees himself as a *thing* in the world, subject to laws; or at least as an obsessive character with virtually no free choice. Sartre imagines a terrible little conversation which illustrates this difference of viewpoint:

'I swear to you that I will do it.'

'Maybe so. You tell me so. I want to believe you. It is indeed possible that you will do it.'

From this conversation, a doubt may arise for the first speaker as to whether he is really in a position to make promises at all. One cannot commit oneself to a future action unless one is conceived as a free agent, with a continuous ability to frame resolutions and stick to them. The ability to do this indeed is one of the most important aspects of human personality. But the second speaker clearly regards the promise as futile, since the behaviour of the promiser is determined quite independently of any promise or undertaking. If I observe a man's behaviour inductively for a long time, as I might observe the behaviour of an ant or a bee, then I feel justified in making inductively based predictions about his conduct. To see oneself as the subject of this kind of inductive prediction is to see oneself suddenly as an object in the natural world, distinguished from other animals only by the ridiculous characteristic of being able to mouth such expressions as 'I promise'. The look of the other is partly important because of the reduction in status which it is thus capable of effecting. And then the question arises of which view is right. Am I right to take my own promises and resolutions seriously; or is he right to regard them as totally irrelevant to the way I will in fact behave? This is analogous to the difficulty of description which I sketched just now. Am I right to regard myself as a complex person with complex motives for doing what I do, or is the other right in regarding me as simply a thief? Which of these points of view is to be taken seriously, if the question arises of how to *treat* me? Sartre is constantly aware of the possibility of a total shift in the point of view, which may radically affect our attitude towards one and the same person. Becoming aware of how I seem to others may, of course, be the origin of bad faith, as we have seen already. To take seriously someone's view of you as incapable of altering your conduct by means of any number of promises or resolutions might lead you to feel that you were determined by your character to go on behaving as you always had; and this would be bad faith. There is, therefore, a perpetual contradiction between a man's actual freedom and his appearance as an object for the other. This is only another version of the familiar debate about responsibility; but it is a version with a peculiar force, since its questions are raised not merely by difficult cases, cases of 'diminished responsibility', or of hypnotism, but by the continuous possibility of a shifting point of view about every aspect of our life.

Other people do not, however, exist merely to look at us and thereby affect our self-awareness. We are constantly entering into various different relations with them, which Sartre sets out to explore. All this part of *Being and Nothingness* has a kind of bewildering power which derives from the intensity of Sartre's imaginative vision of each of us forming his own interpretations of the world, and locked in a constant battle with other people, whom we are obliged to recognize as possessing as much freedom as we do ourselves. For in spite of his repudiation of solipsism, Sartre rejects as bad faith any suggestion that we take over our understanding of the world from other people, that we are taught under what headings to classify it and that we regard it from a common, characteristically human standpoint. We are responsible for our own categories. Each man is therefore left isolated, attempting to sort out his impression of the world for himself. But there is a constant danger of self-deception, as we have seen, even in this attempted sorting out. For the acceptance of any category as necessary or given, the failure to analyse anything, or the mere acceptance of a given way of talking, may all of them be bad faith. This virtual isolation in our own consciousness leads to perpetual failure in our relations with other people. We aim all the time to achieve stability for ourselves, to fill up the emptiness within us, and to take on the status of beings-in-themselves though without losing our consciousness. We try to use other people as means to this self-contradictory end. For instance, if a man is loved by another person, the loving gaze of the other gives him this solid, stable existence which he aims at. But the freedom of the other is an impediment; there is the constant possibility that the gaze may be withdrawn; and furthermore the lover is himself seeking his own stability, and therefore demands the same loving look. There is a struggle therefore between the lovers, each seeking to capture and deny the freedom of the other. But this struggle is in any case self-defeating, since only love or admiration freely given can have the effect of stabilizing the existence of the one loved. To fall in love is therefore to embark on a series of battles which are doomed from the start to futility.

If this is the human situation with regard to the world of external objects and other people, it remains to ask how Sartre thinks we ought actually to behave. Is there anything which it is worth while our trying to be or to do? First, it is essential that we realize that, if there is anything which has value for us, it is a contingent matter. We have created the value for ourselves. The main lesson which we are to learn from the description of our situation is that we must 'repudiate the spirit of seriousness'. Sartre defines the spirit of seriousness as follows: 'It considers values as transcendent, given, independent of human subjectivity, and it transfers the quality of "desirable" from the ontological structure of things to their simple material constitution.' Thus the belief that some things are good in themselves, and the belief that some things are always good because their consequences are desirable, are both equally expressions of this spirit. Above all, non-naturalism in ethics must be abandoned; though ordinary naturalism too is 'serious'. A morality based on such beliefs is a morality of bad faith.

It has obscured all its goals in order to free itself from anguish. Man pursues being blindly by hiding from himself the free project which is this pursuit. He makes himself such that he is *waited for* by all the tasks along his way. Objects are mute demands, and he is nothing in himself but the passive obedience to these demands.

But the fact remains that even though values have no independent existence, we do assign values to things, and regard some things as goals worth pursuing. It is indeed in the word 'goal' that the clue to the concept of value is to be found. You cannot describe something as good in the same way as you can describe it as red. This truth which has so much exercised English moral philosophers is familiar to Sartre as well. If you describe it as good you are uttering a normative expression, and you are suggesting that here is something to be aimed at. Goodness is a quality which does not have existence in the ordinary sense; but to say that something is good or generous or noble is to see it as an instance of a quality which is always to be pursued and will never be reached. This unattainability of the morally perfect is, for Sartre, the reason why properties like goodness have always seemed to moral philosophers both to exist unconditionally and in some sense not to exist at all. It is impossible for any conscious human being not to assign values to things. The essential human characteristic is to form projects and intentions and to pursue aims. To these necessarily and as part of their existence, value attaches. Therefore there is no question of *knowing* that something is good or that it is noble. A project is formed and value 'haunts' this project.

Value is everywhere and nowhere; at the heart of the nihilating relation 'reflection-reflecting' it is present and out of reach, and it is simply lived as the concrete meaning of that lack which makes my present being. . . . Thus reflective consciousness can properly be called moral consciousness since it cannot arise without at the same moment disclosing values.

Now all this may seem disquietingly vague. What Sartre seems to be expressing is a romantic view of morality, according to which there is nothing but the conscience of each of us as a guide, and for each one of us, whatever solitary goal he pursues, he is sure only of never attaining it. And this is, I think, a not unfair estimate of the doctrine in *Being and Nothingness*. But sometimes, particularly in the lecture 'Existentialism is a Humanism', to which I have already referred, Sartre puts forward a theory of morality which has more content and which he expressly compares with the theories of Kant. He there says that if I really aim at my own freedom, which, as a human being, I must necessarily do, I cannot help aiming at the freedom of others. It would be self-contradictory to desire freedom as an end, without universalizing this end, and including in it the freedom of others. It is fairly clear, furthermore, that in this argument he is thinking of freedom not only as the freedom to choose which is the opposite of determinism, but more specifically as political freedom. This view, therefore, could lead to concrete aims, and to a programme of moral and political action not unlike that of Mill and the utilitarians. But it must be admitted that this Kantian-utilitarian view, comforting though it is to come across anything so familiar in the metaphysical jungle, is not really connected in any way with the main part of Sartre's theory. It is given nothing in the way of metaphysical backing; and he does nothing to show that to assign a value to something necessarily entails a universal judgement. We know from the novels, and indeed from everything that Sartre has written, that freedom is in his view the supreme value. But we must admit that it is not wholly clear to what a man is committed if he chooses freedom, or what his alternatives are.

Sartre explains, as an integral part of his whole metaphysical system, how value arises in the world, and how it is that men are so situated that they must always be attempting something which they cannot achieve. But he tells us little about how, for instance, it is possible to argue about matters of value, or how someone would set about showing that one course of action was better than another. There is no formula which can readily be derived from *Being and Nothingness* for deciding what I ought to do; it is difficult even to conceive what form such a decision would take. But it must be remembered that Sartre does not yet suppose himself to have written any kind of moral philosophy. At the very end of *Being and Nothingness* he says that once the moral agent has realized that he is himself the source of all values, 'His freedom will become conscious of itself and reveal itself in anguish as the unique source of value and the emptiness by which the *world* exists.' But the possibility of acting will always be realized only in the context of other people who can also choose and whose choices may affect my own. The question becomes one of trying to find out how far a free agent can escape from his particular situation in his choices; and of how much responsibility he can be brought to accept for being as he is. To these questions Sartre promised to devote another, specifically ethical work.

The whole point of Being + Nothingness is just that no such formula can be given — to ask for one is bad faith

There are two things which may perhaps be said about the form which moral questions must necessarily take, according to existentialist theory. The first is that it is impossible on such a theory sharply to distinguish moral from political questions. It is not *just* an accident of time and place that for Sartre the pressing moral question seems to be 'Shall I join the Communist Party?' Marxist philosophy, like existentialism, insists that morality is a matter not of knowing this or that but of acting; but the action is in accordance with a shared creed. The question for Sartre therefore is always whether the adopting of any shared creed whatever is not going to plunge the believer into bad faith. Though you may freely choose to join the Party, this may well be your last free act. This leads to the second point. Apart from his rather uneasy flirtation with utilitarianism, Sartre seems inclined to think that to give any concrete general rules, or to frame any political programme, is to come perilously near to bad faith. It is impossible not to be involved in the political and social situation in which one finds oneself, but the way through it must be found for each one by himself. It is to this highly romantic, individualist view of morality that Sartre is most deeply committed. If there is any typically moral question it is of the form 'What, here and now, would be the least *phoney* thing for me to choose?'

It is not, therefore, surprising that when the promised new book came[1] it was an intricate attempt to reconcile the individuality of man with his political and social commitments; nor that it should have been written from a Marxist standpoint. For Marxism had come to seem, to Sartre, the only possible philosophy of the twentieth century. This new work can, in the event, hardly be considered as a contribution to moral philosophy at all. Perhaps existentialism, as a form of philosophy, could not survive its own exaggerations and hostility to reason. Philosophy can hardly flourish where reason is, in general, repudiated.

[1] *Critique de la Raison Dialectique.* Paris, 1960.

8
Conclusion

IT IS NOW TIME to attempt some general remarks on the course of the history of ethics in the last sixty years. Is there anything which can profitably be said about all of the different philosophers we have considered in this book? At first sight it may appear that there is one interest which all of them without exception have shared, and that is an interest in refuting ethical naturalism. If hostility could nullify the influence of a philosophical view, then utilitarianism ought by now to be stone dead. The hostility is surprising, particularly in English empirical philosophers, many of whom would in their non-philosophical moments turn out to be utilitarians of an enlightened liberal kind. But this anti-naturalism, although it has been universally a part of recent ethical theories, has taken radically different forms, and the differences are far greater than the similarities.

It has been commonly held that Moore exercised a great influence upon the course of moral philosophy during this century, and this for two reasons. First, he was the inventor of the phrase 'The Naturalistic Fallacy'; and secondly, he directed the attention of philosophers towards the problem of analysing the concept of goodness. As far as the first point goes, Bradley and the other metaphysical philosophers were just as deeply opposed to naturalism as Moore was. Anti-naturalism is not, therefore, in itself a sufficient reason for insisting on the influence of Moore. The name Naturalistic Fallacy it is true, we have all learned from Moore; but I should be inclined to say that we had learned little else. As to the second point, Moore's interests, as I hope to have suggested already, were not in the *language* of morals. He did not care at all how the word 'good' was used. He was interested in what things were good in themselves. He was concerned to show, as all anti-naturalists are, that values are distinct from facts, and that no amount of reflection upon facts, in the ordinary sense, will entitle anyone to make a single value judgement upon them. But he thought that this was because goodness was a special and unique kind of property, the possession of which was different from the possession of other properties. Now if any philosopher is an ethical intuitionist, as Moore was, it is necessary for him to be prepared actually to give examples of those things which have the intuitable property of goodness, or rightness, or whatever it is. Moore was perfectly prepared to do this; in fact, as we have seen, he thought it the easiest thing in the world to do. He told us, in a perfectly straightforward way, what things were as a matter of fact the best things in the world, and therefore what, in general, we should aim at. Sometimes people have objected to recent moral philosophy that it has been, at least in England and America, uncommitted; that it has taken no sides, and given no guidance about how to behave. People who have made this complaint cannot have read the philosophy of Moore. The other intuitionists also told us what things were obligatory, but unfortunately they, for the most part, failed to hold our attention. They cheated by telling us to do only the things we would have done anyway, like returning books we have borrowed. They did not tell us how to live, or how to treat other people in serious matters. But from *Principia Ethica* we could, if we tried, derive this information. This difference between Moore and the other intuitionists brings out, I think, the real reason why we continue to read *Principia Ethica*, and why in the history of this period of moral philosophy Moore looms so large. The reason is that the book is so good and so eccentric. Moore dominates us through its pages just as he dominated his contemporaries in Cambridge. There is no comparable book on ethics in this century. But to be great is not the same as to be influential.

There is one respect, however, in which subsequent philo-sophers did follow Moore. Whereas Bradley, following Hegelian,

and ultimately Kantian models of ethical theory, regarded
human choice as the only proper subject matter of morals, and
further, thought of choice as something which must essentially
be viewed from inside, from behind the eyes of the agent,
Moore and moral philosophers after him were concerned only
secondarily with choices. Their main interest was in judging
things to be good or bad, right or wrong. The central question
became 'What is a moral judgement?' It was inevitable that
Moore himself should adopt this standpoint, since his concern
(1)   was with the property of goodness, which was a property of
things in the external world, there to be discovered. It was
states of consciousness which were good, and it did not matter
whose state of consciousness it was; all could equally come up
for judgement.

It was equally natural that Ayer and the logical positivists
should adopt the same standpoint. Their concern was to mark
(2)   off scientific from non-scientific discourse, statements of fact
from pseudo-statements which purported to, but did not, state
facts. Their attention was therefore naturally drawn to the differences between statements such as 'the boy is a diabetic' and
'the boy is a good influence in the house'. Once again the proper
function of moral philosophy appeared to be to discuss moral
judgements, though now in a new way.

From the positivists, and the heyday of the emotive theory,
(3)   it was, as I hope I have shown, only a short step to the post-war
linguistic analyses which issued mainly from Oxford. Here
again the point of view is the same. Anti-naturalism still characterizes this philosophy as well; but it has moved very far from
the anti-naturalism of Moore. What distinguishes a moral from
a non-moral judgement is now not the kind of property which
they each call attention to, but the logic of the words used in
the statement of each. Ethical judgements are seen as a sub-
class of value judgements in general, and the most general form
of the question raised by these philosophers is 'What is it to
evaluate things?' or 'What is the difference between evaluating
things and describing them?'

It may be thought that I am unfair to some philosophers of
the last ten years; they have not all, it may be urged, concentrated so exclusively on the judging and assessing, the grading

and marking aspect of morality. After all, Hare regarded moral judgements as imperatives, and the point of an imperative is that it should galvanize someone into activity. It is not just a spectator's judgement of the scene. Nowell-Smith, equally, maintained that many moral words, at least much of the time, were specifically intended to indicate that something ought to be done about the situation to which they were applied. (One of his examples was the word 'weed' which was supposed to suggest the necessity of action in any keen gardener.) I do not deny that these philosophers, like Hume and Berkeley before them, recognized that the language which we use about things may affect our attitude towards these things, and therefore even our actions. But this does not seem to me to constitute a real difference between them and the emotive theorists. Their interest was still concentrated upon the actual words used in the framing of what they called ethical propositions. An ethical proposition may, it is true, take various forms, but there was supposed to be a connexion between all the different forms it might take, and this connexion lay in the logical characteristics of the words used. The differences between 'I ought to do this' and 'This is right' or 'This is good' were not really represented as serious or important differences. Therefore, in the end, it did not make very much difference whether cases of personal choice were taken as examples, or cases of public advice, or cases of judgement after the event. The same analysis would do, with a few adjustments, for all the cases. The standpoint was still that of the judge or the schoolmaster, even if sometimes the judgement was passed or the report written with an eye to the future.

This, then, seems to me the most important way in which, whether under the influence of Moore or not, later philosophers have followed his practice. There is one other less important feature common to their writings. Moore was convinced that *goodness* was the central concept of ethics and, apart from an extension to cover 'ought', 'right', and 'duty', most philosophers of the last sixty years have agreed with him. There is a small and general set of concepts which have been singled out for treatment in books about ethics. It is a great pity, however, to concentrate on this small group of words, especially as they are not words which, with the exception of 'duty', have any particular relevance to ethics. If it is the logic of ethical language which is interesting, then it might have been better to start to analyse some words which appear only in ethical contexts, instead of insisting on first of all examining these extremely general and virtually contentless words. Admittedly 'ought' and 'right' come into our moral vocabulary, but they do not exhaust it. As for 'good', I doubt whether it even comes in very much except in the pages of books about moral philosophy.

One of the consequences of treating ethics as the analysis of ethical language is, as I have suggested earlier, that it leads to the increasing triviality of the subject. This is not a general criticism of linguistic analysis, but only of this method applied to ethics. In ethics, alone among the branches of philosophical study, the subject matter is not so much the categories which we use to describe or to learn about the world, as our own impact upon the world, our relation to other people and our attitude to our situation and our life. We do need to categorize and to describe, even in the sphere of morals, but we should still exist as moral agents even if we seldom did so; and therefore the subject matter of ethics would still exist. How we describe the world cannot be the primary concern of moral philosophers; and it is an evasion to say that by distinguishing between evaluating and describing, moral philosophers have avoided assimilating ethics to epistemology. Evaluating is not the distinctive function of moral agents either. Deliberating, wishing, hating, loving, choosing; these are things which characterize us as people, and therefore as moral agents, and these are the things to which the emotive theory and its later developments paid insufficient attention.

One aspect of this trivializing of the subject is the refusal of moral philosophers in England to commit themselves to any moral opinions. They have for the most part fallen in happily with the positivist distinction between moral philosophers, who analyse the logic of moral discourse, and moralists, who practise it. It follows that they are inclined to believe that, in theory at least, absolutely anything could count as a moral opinion, or a moral principle, provided it was framed in the way laid down for such principles, and used, as they are used, to guide conduct. It would be generally agreed that some opinions might be outrageous, and some principles harmful, but where we get our principles and opinions from, how we should decide between them, and what would be an example of a good one—these things they will not tell us, for to do so would be actually to express a moral opinion. This caution derives, as it is easy to see, at least in part from the obsessive fear of naturalism. If it were possible for these philosophers to say that some moral principles are derived from what people actually want, or desire in the long run, then they could say what these principles were without appearing to be dogmatic, or to be merely voicing their private preferences. Hume and Mill would have been happy to give any number of examples of good moral principles, and to derive each of them directly or indirectly from some general desire for security or human happiness. But this would be to destroy the autonomy of ethics, or so they say. Thus the concentration upon the most general kind of evaluative language, combined with the fear of committing the naturalistic fallacy, has led too often to discussions of grading fruit, or choosing fictitious games equipment, and ethics as a serious subject has been left further and further behind.

But I believe that the most boring days are over. I cannot risk much speculation about the future, but there is no doubt that in at least three different but related ways an interest in the subject matter of ethics is reviving. First, under the general influence of Wittgenstein, it is increasingly recognized that in order to discuss any subject properly, it is necessary to see the language which is appropriate to it actually at work. This leads to the consideration of a more interesting set of concepts than the right and the good. Virtues and vices may now be considered, as well as feelings, scruples, desires, intentions, and other psychological phenomena. Secondly, an increasing interest in the question of what specially characterizes a moral as opposed to any other evaluative judgement, is leading philosophers at least to reopen the question of ethical naturalism. Is it after all perhaps not so self-evident that empirical considerations about what does people good and what does them harm are irrelevant to deciding what is a moral principle and what is not? In this connexion I should call attention to two very persuasive articles by Philippa Foot, in *Mind*, 1958, and the *Proceedings of the Aristotelian Society*, 1958, which display both the tendencies I have mentioned, and which have aroused great interest.

Finally, there is at least the possibility that we may in England learn a little from the Continent. I do not for a moment mean to suggest that we should all become Hegelian metaphysicians. That would be both undesirable and anyway impossible. Philosophy progresses, and it has now progressed beyond the stage at which a philosopher can simply invent a system which pleases him and by means of which he can explain everything in the universe. But even if total explanations are no longer possible, that is no reason why we should not still look at human beings in general in their context in the world. If we do this, it is likely that the most important thing about them should appear to us, as it did to Kant, to Hegel, to Bradley, and to Sartre, to be their capacity for acting spontaneously, and choosing between alternatives; for making and keeping resolutions, for regretting their decisions and rationally changing their minds, for feeling guilt and feeling pride in their achievements. If this capacity is what makes morality possible, then it should surely be in this group of phenomena that moral philosophers should, at least partly, interest themselves. I think that in the past, philosophers have been too much concerned with moral *theories* to pay very much attention to how people actually decide, or what moral decisions are really like. For instance, it has too often been suggested, without sufficient support, that all moral decisions must be decisions *on principle*, or decisions to do something *because it is a duty*. Reading Sartre, if it taught us nothing else, might perhaps open our eyes to the suggestion that not all moral decisions are of this kind; and indeed that sometimes to do something on the supposition that it is a duty, waiting to be fulfilled, would be bad faith.

Moral philosophy might in this way properly include both description of the complexities of actual choices and actual decisions, and also discussion of what would count as reasons for making this or that decision. I believe that this is what philosophers are beginning gradually to do. It is impossible to predict what kind of books they will actually write. But the examples which they contain will necessarily have to be long, complicated, and realistic. I think that the days of shouting to revive the fainting man, and the days of grading apples, are over. Moral philosophy will be much more difficult, perhaps much more embarrassing, to write than it has been recently. but it will be far more interesting to read.

Short Bibliography

THE FOLLOWING LIST includes those books and articles discussed in the text and several others which seem to be essential reading for anyone interested in the ethical writings of this period. There is, however, no claim to completeness.

All books listed are published in London unless otherwise indicated.

I. BOOKS

F. H. Bradley. *Ethical Studies.* 2nd edition, Oxford University Press, 1927.

G. E. Moore. *Principia Ethica.* Cambridge University Press, 1903. *Ethics.* Home University Library, Thornton Butterworth, 1912; Oxford Paperbacks University Series, Oxford University Press, 1966.

W. D. Ross. *The Right and the Good.* Oxford University Press, 1930. *The Foundations of Ethics.* Oxford University Press, 1939.

H. A. Pritchard. *Moral Obligation: Essays and Lectures.* Oxford University Press, 1949.

E. F. Carritt. *Theory of Morals.* Oxford University Press, 1928.

H. W. B. Joseph. *Some Problems in Ethics.* Oxford University Press, 1931.

C. D. Broad. *Ethics and the History of Philosophy.* Routledge & Kegan Paul, 1952.

C. K. Ogden and I. A. Richards. *The Meaning of Meaning.* Kegan Paul, London, 1923.

A. J. Ayer. *Language, Truth and Logic.* Gollancz, 1936; 2nd edition, 1946.

C. L. Stevenson. *Ethics and Language.* Yale University Press, 1945.

A. C. Ewing. *The Definition of Good.* Routledge & Kegan Paul, 1947.

G. Ryle. *The Concept of Mind.* Hutchinson University Library, 1949.

A. N. Prior. *Logic and the Basis of Ethics*. Oxford University Press, 1949.

S. E. Toulmin. *An Examination of the Place of Reason in Ethics*. Cambridge, 1950.

R. M. Hare. *The Language of Morals*. Oxford University Press, 1952.
Freedom and Reason. Oxford University Press, 1963.

L. Wittgenstein. *Philosophical Investigations*. Translated G. E. M Anscombe. Blackwell, Oxford, 1953.

Iris Murdoch. *Sartre*. Bowes & Bowes, Cambridge, 1953.

P. H. Nowell-Smith. *Ethics*. Penguin Books, 1954; Blackwell, Oxford, 1957.

G. E. M. Anscombe. *Intention*. Blackwell, Oxford, 1957.

J.-P. Sartre. *Being and Nothingness*. Translated Hazel E. Barnes. Philosophical Library of New York, 1956; Methuen, 1957.

K. Baier. *The Moral Point of View, a Rational Basis of Ethics*. Ithaca, N.Y., 1958.

A. Farrer. *The Freedom of the Will*. Black, 1958.

A. Montefiore. *A Modern Introduction to Moral Philosophy*. Routledge & Kegan Paul, 1958.

S. Hampshire. *Thought and Action*. Chatto & Windus, 1959.

A. W. H. Adkins. *Merit and Responsibility*. Oxford University Press, 1960.

M. Singer. *Generalizations in Ethics*. Eyre & Spottiswoode, 1963.

J. L. Austin. *Philosophical Papers*. Oxford University Press, 1960.

Antony Kenny. *Action, Emotion and Will*. Routledge & Kegan Paul, 1963.

Charles Taylor. *The Explanation of Behaviour*. Routledge & Kegan Paul, 1964.

G. J. Warnock. *Contemporary Moral Philosophy*. Macmillan, 1966.

II. ARTICLES

C. L. Stevenson. 'The Emotive Meaning of Ethical Terms'. *Mind*, 1937.
'Ethical Judgments and Avoidability'. *Mind*, 1938.
'Persuasive Definitions'. *Mind*, 1938.

J. N. Findlay. 'Morality by Convention'. *Mind*, 1944.
'The Justification of Attitudes'. *Mind*, 1954.

P. F. Strawson. 'Ethical Intuitionism'. *Philosophy*, 1949.
'Freedom and Resentment'. Henrietta Hertz Lecture at the British Academy, 1962.

J. O. Urmson. 'On Grading'. *Mind*, 1950.

P. R. Foot. 'Moral Arguments'. *Mind*, 1958.

  'Moral Beliefs'. *Proceedings of the Aristotelian Society*, 1958.

  'When is a principle a moral principle?' *Proceedings of the Aristotelian Society*, Supplementary Volume 28.

Index